Victory at Poitiers

Other titles in the Campaign Chronicles series:

Victory at Poitiers

The Black Prince and the Medieval Art of War

Christian Teutsch

Campaign Chronicle
Series Editor

Christopher Summerville

Pen & Sword
MILITARY

First published in Great Britain in 2010 by
Pen & Sword Military
an imprint of
Pen & Sword Books Ltd
47 Church Street
Barnsley
South Yorkshire
S70 2AS

Copyright © Christian Teutsch 2010

ISBN 978-1-84415-932-1

The right of Christian Teutsch to be identified as Author of this Work has been
asserted by him in accordance with the Copyright, Designs and Patents Act 1988.

A CIP catalogue record for this book is available from the British Library.

Typeset in 11/13.5pt Garamond by
Mac Style, Beverley, East Yorkshire

Printed and bound in the UK by
CPI

Pen & Sword Books Ltd incorporates the imprints of Pen & Sword Aviation, Pen
& Sword Maritime, Pen & Sword Military, Wharncliffe Local History, Pen and
Sword Select, Pen and Sword Military Classics, Leo Cooper, Remember When,
Seaforth Publishing and Frontline Publishing.

For a complete list of Pen & Sword titles please contact
PEN & SWORD BOOKS LIMITED
47 Church Street, Barnsley, South Yorkshire, S70 2AS, England
E-mail: enquiries@pen-and-sword.co.uk
Website: www.pen-and-sword.co.uk

Contents

—◦(◦)◦—

List of Maps

—◦—

Maps

Introduction

Now, sirs, though we be but a small company as in regard to the puissance of our enemies, let us not be abashed therefore; for the victory lieth not in the multitude of people, but whereas God will send it. If it fortune that the journey be ours, we shall be the most honoured people of all the world; and if we die in our right quarrel, I have the king my father and brethren, and also ye have good friends and kinsmen; these shall revenge us. Therefore, sirs, for God's sake I require you do your devoirs this day; for if God be pleased and Saint George, this day ye shall see me a good knight.

– Edward the Black Prince immediately before Poitiers, as reported by Jean Froissart

Edward sat astride his riding horse, preserving his destrier for its designated role – that moment in battle when the young prince might lead a heavy cavalry charge in all its glory against the fleeing French forces arrayed before him. But that was not how this battle would begin. The chronicler Geoffrey le Baker reports that as soon as scouts brought word that King Jean II had not only finally caught up with the English invasion force, but had formed his men into battle in anticipation of a fight, Edward dismounted and directed his fellow knights to do the same. Today the Black Prince would fight on foot – his 6,000 against the French 14,000.

Edward, with the forces under his immediate command, was occupying a hillock on what now became the English left flank. Less than a half mile to his right front he could see the lead elements of the French assault, under Marshal Clermont, bursting through the thick hedgeline. This group of elite horsemen had seen the English forces consolidating and had determined to assault the English longbowmen to break up their lines and prevent them massing their fire and repeating that tactic that had so devastated the French mounted assaults on the field of Crécy-en-Ponthieu ten years before. However, the hedge served to disrupt the mounted charge, and as the Frenchmen broke through the few gaps, the prepositioned longbowmen fired at point-blank range. Froissart reports that they 'struck terror into the hearts of the French, for the rain of arrows was so continuous and so thick that the French did not know where to turn to avoid them'.

But the battle was far from won. Arrows were not as effective against the next charge, led by Clermont's co-commander of the French vanguard, Marshal d' Audrehem. His battalion, which attacked along a route parallel to Clermont's but barely a quarter mile from Edward's location, enjoyed much more success at first, but eventually it, too, fell victim to the superiority of the English missiles. Soon after, the second division of the French army, 4,000 dismounted men-at-arms under the command of the Dauphin, had crossed the fields and were aimed directly at the prince's division, which had not yet been engaged. Behind the Dauphin's division, out of sight due to the undulating terrain – but definitely not beyond the notice of Edward – were the third and fourth French divisions, under the Duke of Orléans and King Jean II, respectively. These two units alone outnumbered the meagre English forces present, and included some of the most distinguished knights of the realm. And here was young Edward, outnumbered, backed against a river, several days' march from friendly lines. Was this the fight that he had hoped for or was it one that (much to his dread) had been forced upon him?

What had brought the Black Prince to this point? Why had he invaded France? Why had he brought such a paltry force? Did he really want to face Jean in battle? And what did he ultimately hope to achieve? Observers and historians have wrestled with these questions for nearly seven centuries. While contemporaries overwhelmingly held the young tactician in the highest regard, in the modern age his critics have outnumbered his admirers, and have almost universally underestimated Edward as a military commander.

Far from being chased to Poitiers and forced into a battle, Edward had lured his father's rival into this fight. His entire strategy for this campaign rested upon his ability to draw the French king into being the one to attack. He did not have enough men – the English *never* had enough men – to face the French in a set-piece battle on even terms. But there was no need for Edward to seek such a fight now. He had driven his army through the heart of France, taken what he wanted, despoiled what he didn't, and lured the wearer of his father's crown into a position where he would be compelled to attack the 6,000 English and Gascons or go home in disgrace.

Jean did not want to be the attacker – to assume the tactical offence – any more than did Edward. While neither to this point had *extensive* command experience, each could draw upon sufficient examples from the recent past to have gained an appreciation of the inherent strength of tactical defence. Edward, in particular, learned from the English experience at Bannockburn in

Introduction

1314, Halidon Hill in 1333, at both Crécy and Neville's Cross in 1346, and at the siege of Calais in 1346–1347. From these campaigns he knew that: (1) reluctant armies could be brought to battle given the right incentive; (2) these battles were not only more likely to occur if the enemy trusted too heavily in his own weight of numbers, but that victory was more dependent upon tactical than numerical superiority; and, (3) that battle as 'the final arbiter' could empower a kingdom of lesser economy and population to overcome a stronger rival.

Poitiers was to be Edward's opportunity to apply all he had learned, and to increase not only his personal glory, but that of the Plantagenet empire. But to appreciate what the Black Prince hoped to gain on 19 September 1356, on the obstacle-studded field straddling the Maupertuis in central France, one must first understand how men of his day engaged in combat, and why England and France found themselves locked in a war spanning not years but lifetimes.

Medieval Warfare

T his book does not attempt to explain in great detail such complex matters of historical debate as feudal relationships, daily medieval life, or systems of military services and pay, but it does hope to provide sufficient descriptions of key concepts to permit an understanding of the era of the Black Prince. And in this discussion it must always be remembered that individuals living in the medieval era were not merely modern people inserted into a 'less advanced' time. They held values and beliefs just as foreign to contemporary Western society as the most disparate contemporary cultures do today. But in these values and beliefs we can also detect some points of similarity, just as there exist some shared principles that traverse oceans and continents in any time period.

The People: Warfare for the Three Estates

An army – regardless of the age in which it fights, the purpose for which it is raised, and the arms with which it is equipped – has no more critical components than the soldiers who fill its ranks and the commanders who lead them. It would be absurd to attempt to describe the 'typical' composition of a medieval army, even if one were to limit the discussion to a particular region, such as England or France, because of the sheer extent of what is generally considered the Middle Ages. The period arguably, extends from the beginning of the ninth century AD to the end of the fifteenth, framed at its inception by Charlemagne's coronation on Christmas Day, AD 800, and at its end with the termination of the *Reconquista* at the battle of Valencia on 2 January, 1492. That Christopher Columbus ushered in the Age of Exploration that same year only adds to the significance of this date. Additionally, the date falls neatly between the final battle of the Hundred Years War, Castillon in 1453, which is also the same year as the Turkish conquest of Constantinople and the resultant fall of the Eastern Roman empire, and Martin Luther's advancement of the Protestant Reformation by nailing his *95 Theses* to the church door at Wittenberg in 1517. The end of the hegemony of the Catholic Church in Europe ushered in an immensely turbulent era of political change.

Victory at Poitiers

Most historians agree that the Middle Ages ended sometime around the last years of the fifteenth century, but the start date is much more contentious. The traditional proposal of AD 476, corresponding with Germanic warlord Odoacer's sack of Rome, is not an entirely satisfactory date. French historian Henri Pirenne convincingly argues in his momentous 1935 work, *Mohammed and Charlemagne*, that the Roman world of antiquity by the fifth century AD was no longer as centred on the 'immortal city' so much as the far-flung institutions it had created, particularly with regard to commerce. Only with the advent of Islam and its hugely successful eighth-century expansion, which deprived former Roman colonies of free use of the Mediterranean, did the last vestiges of the empire disappear from daily life. Coinciding with what thus became a demographic shift to the north, away from the Muslim-controlled Mediterranean and into the heart of Europe, was the advent of the iron stirrup. Though there existed no direct causal relationship between the introduction of the iron stirrup into Western culture sometime around AD 700 and the rise of what has come to be known as the *feudal system*, this and related technologies certainly contributed to the dominance of the class of warrior nobility that has since represented the medieval era.

It is convenient for modern historians to organize members of medieval society neatly into well-defined groups, normally according to the roles each played in society. But these distinctions are far from a purely modern construct. Around the turn of the first millennium, Bishop Adalbero of Laon separated society into three classes: *sacerdotes* (those who pray), *milites* (those who fight), and *laborarii* (those who work). Thus the three estates were born. The third estate, the peasant class, comprised the vast majority of the population of Western Europe – estimates range from 90 to 95 per cent. Nevertheless, the first and second estates held the power. During this period, revenue from land was the basis of power, and those who worked the land were beholden to those for whom they toiled. Ownership was what mattered, not labour.

Fourteenth-century English peasants, however – due to unforeseeable consequences – profited greatly from two otherwise catastrophic events. While the third of the population that suffered the ravages of the first outbreaks of the Black Death in 1348–1349 clearly were not beneficiaries of the epidemic, those who survived found themselves in the heretofore unimaginable position of being in high demand. Most of those who had felt the full effects of the Black Death were those who were too poor to evacuate the disease-infested cities; the wealthy among the aristocracy and clergy often emigrated to the supposedly cleaner air of country estates. The poor who did survive, however, now found themselves in a position of great opportunity. In many places, despite legislative attempts to stem the trend, landlords were forced to pay higher wages and

6

demand fewer services of their workers. Small landowners abandoned fringe land holdings on the margins of their communities, ceased attempts at reclaiming marshes, the weald and the highlands, and assumed control of long-cultivated properties that produced higher yields with less work. Landlords eagerly welcomed the new arrivals as replacements for tenants lost to the Black Death. Without new tenants, the lands lay fallow, and owners found themselves unable to pay their own rents to their lords. Thus the Black Death improved the financial standing of many of its survivors among the peasant class, but little had been done to augment their place in society. In fact, in some ways it had deteriorated in the years since the outbreak, as nobles latched on to instances of post-plague opportunism to label peasants greedy and self-serving. Open rebellions – such as the one led by Wat Tyler in 1381 – only cemented the stigma.

But the other 'catastrophe' of the period did much to promote peasants' collective standing in society. The Hundred Years War – disastrous, perhaps, to the royal economies of both England and France – actually had some positive effects for individual peasants, merchants and nobles. Many argue that peasants were elevated in conjunction with the rise of the English longbow. This weapon of the masses, deriving its power from its massed effect, cannot but have increased the yeoman's value on the field of battle, breaking the long-time hegemony of nobles in that arena. English kings – forever short of cash and lusty for war – found the longbow a bargain. It could be cheaply attained, cheaply manned, and cheaply resupplied. Additionally, and perhaps most importantly, it proved devastatingly effective when massed against targets ill-equipped to defend against its powers of penetration.

While paying due reverence to the weapon, we must be careful not to attribute to it alone the many English victories between 1330 and 1430. It was the application of the longbow – not its mere existence – that delivered success. Wisely applied, it brought so much success, the venerated Sir Charles Oman writes, that: 'Edward the Black Prince and his father [who] regarded themselves as the flower of chivalry [...] would have been horrified had they realized that their own tactics were going to make chivalrous warfare impossible.'[1] I leave it to the reader to determine whether the English commanders were so oblivious to the implications of their chosen tactics. But one must recognize that the longbow of itself did not win a single engagement. No weapon's worth is independent of the skill with which it is wielded. Edward I, Edward III, the Black Prince and Henry V each understood and demonstrated some level of mastery of their national weapon. Others did not, and their names are scarcely remembered in the annals of warfare. Skilled commanders, not technological advances, win battle and wars. It is to them that the honours must be given.

Victory at Poitiers

Just as the longbow is not the sole source of victory for Edward III and his successors, neither is it the sole basis for the rise of the fourteenth-century English peasant. The Hundred Years War, which brought about so much fame for the weapon, also should be credited with the growth and empowerment of the English Parliament. When English kings required money, as they ceaselessly did, they had few alternatives but to turn to their nobles and request revenues. This bargaining often resulted in the allowance of concessions of royal power. Having gained the right to tax, Parliament eventually gained the right to legislate. The more the English kings sought to wage war, the more money they required. Campaigns like Crécy, Neville's Cross, the *Grande Chevauchée* of 1355 and Poitiers were anomalies – the spoils almost paying for expenditures made at their outset. More common was the campaign that spent much and gained little. With each of these the king had to curry political and economic favour from Parliament, resulting in a surrender of royal prerogative in exchange for a furthering of royal agenda. And with each of these failed campaigns the power of Parliament, and eventually of the middling ranks of society, grew.

The first estate, the clergy, were not all pacifists, as so often portrayed. The 'Peace of God', result of the Synod of Charroux in 989, is often cited as outlawing attacks made upon clergy. Close reading, however, reveals that the only clergy protected by this ordinance were those who were not armoured or bearing arms:

> Anathema against those who injure clergymen. If anyone attacks, seizes, or beats a priest, deacon, or any other clergyman, who is not bearing arms (shield, sword, coat of mail, or helmet), but is going along peacefully or staying in the house, the sacrilegious person shall be excommunicated and cut off from the church, unless he makes satisfaction, or unless the bishop discovers that the clergyman brought it upon himself by his own fault.[2]

Clearly, the priesthood had among its ranks men who at least sometimes engaged in warfare, even at the time of the Synod of Charroux, over a century before the establishment of the first military orders. This should not be surprising when one considers that the upper ranks of the clergy were filled with the brothers of the most famous knights of Christendom. These boys grew up in the same martial culture as the future barons, princes and kings. Some of the clergy even led armies, as the Archbishop of York did at the battle of Neville's Cross. Bishops were even more commonly commanders further east, on the medieval German frontier.

But what of the secular knights? The warriors about whom we read so much, and who, for so many of us, represent the very picture of medieval warfare? At the time of the Hundred Years War, knights raised the armies, led the armies, and paid the armies. These are all activities we can track with surviving documents. Calls to arms record for us the rallying of troops. The rolls tell us who was at the battle, and financial records detail the payment of soldiers. We have, however, no documentation of knights leading that other critical facet of military service – training. There is no evidence of medieval commanders leading large-scale training manoeuvres as we would expect a modern army to conduct. They probably did not occur. Training was conducted primarily at the individual level, though certainly men grew accustomed to fighting alongside one another, particularly during eras of persistent conflict. It is this question of how tactics evolved that is most interesting, and perhaps hardest to determine.

The Operations: The Conduct of War

When considering warfare, perhaps one's first thoughts turn to the battlefield. In truth, it is curious that that which is most frequently referred to as 'conventional warfare' – meaning open, set-piece battle between full-time military personnel, usually in uniform, sponsored and led by a state or other level of government – has during very few periods of history been 'the convention'. Most periods of warfare are composed of 'low intensity conflict' not great battles. Many historians have noted this truth, but generally do so with the caveat that, at some time around the advent of gunpowder weapons, commanders began an obsession with 'decisive battle' – intimating that, at times previous to this, during the medieval era for example, commanders preferred devastation and siege warfare. In the 'Western military tradition', however, it has been the general trend that when multiple superpowers are at odds, they tend to be reluctant to commit to a truly decisive battle; whereas, when a distinct hegemony exists, that lone superpower seeks to play to its own strengths, imposing itself on its neighbours through the projection of conventional military might. Competent commanders never seek to attack without advantage.

There are two obvious objections to this proposal: counter-examples certainly exist, and, when considered, the theory may appear counter-intuitive. It cannot be reiterated enough when considering military history that commanders generally seek to fight at the times, against the enemies, and by the means, that offer the greatest likelihood of victory. A dominant conventional force, despite its inherent strength, is most effective when pitted against a lesser conventional force. Examples throughout history up to the present day confirm this maxim. A conventional force, no matter how great its numbers or how advanced its technology, often finds itself ill-prepared to face an insurgent force, or even a conventional one that is unwilling to fight. For this reason, commanders of conventional forces tend to prefer to face neither comparable armies, which they may not be able to defeat without suffering devastating losses themselves, nor 'unconventional forces' that would, by design, minimize the effectiveness of 'conventional' tactics.

To put this discussion in terms of warfare of the fourteenth century, a wealthy state with sufficient manpower would seek to deploy a large force composed overwhelmingly of heavy cavalry. The ideal military target for such an army would be a smaller formation of like structure. Certainly a pack of untrained and ill-armed peasants would be easier to rout than a well-organized army, but its defeat would gain for the victors neither the acclaim nor the strategic advantage that they sought. Only by vanquishing a viable threat could the aggressor be credited with a legitimate victory.

Unwilling or unable to conduct an effective military campaign, a state, then as now, might seek non-military means of conflict resolution. Alternatively, it might trust in superior tactics or technology to compensate for its other deficiencies. England – inferior in numbers and wealth to France – worked to mobilize its economy and to optimize its tactics to defeat its powerful neighbour. But the French, too, were able to make strategic and technological advancements that, in the end, enabled them to win the war. The Hundred Years War was a conflict wrought with political intrigue and bounded by military innovation. It began with the longbow and ended with gunpowder artillery. When one considers that the English mastered the first and the French best integrated the second, it is not difficult to explain England's initial success and France's ultimate victory. The significance of the innovations, however, does not lie in their technological merit, but rather in what their application to warfare reveals about the men and societies that embraced them.

Professor Clifford Rogers, in his essay, 'Edward III and the Dialectics of Strategy',[3] demonstrates that, despite the too often portrayed image of medieval commanders being completely devoid of any capacity for strategic thought, Edward III learned from the martial experiences of his youth and applied these lessons to his own campaigns in France, specifically during the 1346 actions, culminating in the battle of Crécy. Historians have for too long criticized both Edward III and his son, the Black Prince, for making poor strategic decisions, or have discounted the English victories at Crécy, Poitiers and Agincourt as French-imposed engagements upon an overextended and retreating English raiding force. As Rogers demonstrates, however, Edward III had witnessed first-hand the capabilities of a raiding force given the correct composition and the benefit of tactical defence. When, during the first year of his reign, the young Edward III's lands were invaded by Scottish horsemen, he sought to engage them in battle to punish them for having pillaged the north country. He caught up with them at the River Wear only to find them arrayed for battle in an unassailable position on a hilltop overlooking the river crossing. Remembering the fate of his father's army at Bannockburn, he wisely chose not to assault the Scottish *schiltrons* while they were at such an advantage. Learning that they could not be coaxed from their position, he had no choice but to forego combat, and thus allow the Scottish raiding party to escape with many English subjects' possessions and much of the English king's pride. When, nearly twenty years later, Prince Edward was planning his own *chevauchée*, this time into France, he knew exactly how best to draw King Jean into a disadvantageous battle or disgrace him for refusing to fight.

The Hundred Years War

T he Hundred Years War, a conflict generally considered to have spanned the years 1337–1453, was predominantly a contest between England and France, the two great kingdoms of Western Europe. Key roles were also played by many smaller powers as well, including: Scotland, Burgundy, Flanders, Navarre, Castile, and various German states. Though the fighting technically began during the reigns of Edward III and Philip VI, the war actually had its foundations centuries earlier, and an examination of its root causes reveals the intricately interwoven nature of the emergence of the two kingdoms throughout the High and Late Middle Ages.

Before he was William the Conqueror, king of a united England, he was the bastard from Normandy, a French-born, French-speaking illegitimate son of Robert I, Duke of Normandy. When he defeated Harold Godwinson at the battle of Hastings in 1066 and subsequently laid claim to much of his new island home, he did not abandon his Continental interests. Despite the relative ignominy of his birth, he was his father's only son, and as such, his heir. He succeeded his father in 1037, aged 7, was knighted eight years later, and at 24 married Mathilda of Flanders, beginning what would be a lengthy relationship between the two natural enemies of France. By the time he earned his famous sobriquet, he had already seized the county of Maine, establishing the roots of the Angevin empire. Thus, in 1066, William's holdings straddled the Channel and posed a formidable rivalry to the kings of France.

In 1137, exactly 200 years before the start of the Hundred Years War, Eleanor's father, William X of Aquitaine, died. That summer she married Louis, heir apparent to the French throne. When Louis VI, his father, died that same year, Louis VII and Eleanor were crowned king and queen of France. After fifteen years of marriage Eleanor had provided two daughters but no male heirs for Louis. Their marriage was annulled. Since Aquitaine had been Eleanor's dowry, she kept it after the marriage dissolved. Within two months she had remarried, this time to Henry Plantagenet of Anjou, who accordingly was given the title Duke of Aquitaine, though Eleanor still held the Continental possessions in her own right. Two years later, in 1154, Henry was crowned

Henry II of England, and Eleanor wore a queen's crown for the second time. Thus, Louis VII suddenly found that, in a very brief time, he had not only lost his queen and his largest fiefdom, but had lost them both to his bitter rival, the king of England.

Henry II was succeeded in turn by two of his surviving sons, the famous Richard 'Lionheart' and John 'Lackland'. Richard, the renowned crusader, died without heir so the throne passed to John, who had the great misfortune of being a notoriously inept king ruling at the same time as a distinctively adept rival monarch, Philip Augustus of France. The latter managed to strip England of some of its key Continental possessions, including Normandy and Anjou. In 1259, John's son, Henry III, consented to the Treaty of Paris, which completely abrogated any future claims to the lands of the Angevin empire: Normandy, Anjou, Maine and Poitou. Henry was able to retain Aquitaine (also referred to as Gascony or Guienne), but only as a vassal to St Louis, then king of France. Henry III's son, Edward I 'Longshanks', spent most of his reign consolidating the island kingdom. He conquered Wales and led repeated campaigns in an attempt to subjugate the Scots, finally dying while on campaign in 1307. The only military activity he attempted on the Continent had been the aborted operations of the 1290s. These had followed Philip IV's seizure of Gascony, prompted by Edward's refusal to journey to France to take an oath of fealty as Philip's vassal. Perhaps the aspect of Edward I's reign that most contributed to the outbreak of the Hundred Years War was the burgeoning relationship between Scotland and France, England's two most natural enemies. The British Isles were, however, well on their way to unification and Gascony was, for the time being, securely in English hands.

Edward I's successor, Edward II, did not advance English affairs on any front. He was no soldier, and proved this repeatedly against the Scots in campaigns that reversed much his father had accomplished. Oman characterizes his generalship as 'unskilful, almost insane'.[4] In Gascony, his headstrong lieutenants conducted strategically disruptive campaigns against the French, causing further agitation in an already precarious situation. Edward II's relationship with his barons was so disastrous that they eventually removed him from the throne in a most disgraceful fashion.

With the accession of Edward III to the throne in 1327, however, England's fortunes began to change, though this was not immediately apparent. One of the young king's first acts was to sign the Treaty of Paris in March of 1327, which essentially halted all actions in Gascony and paid an indemnity to Charles IV for the destruction Edward's English vassals had caused in the region.[5] The following year, however, Charles IV, the last Capetian king, died without heir. Edward's mother, Isabella, was Charles' sister. Thus, Edward III was of more direct lineage than the other primary claimant to the French throne, Charles'

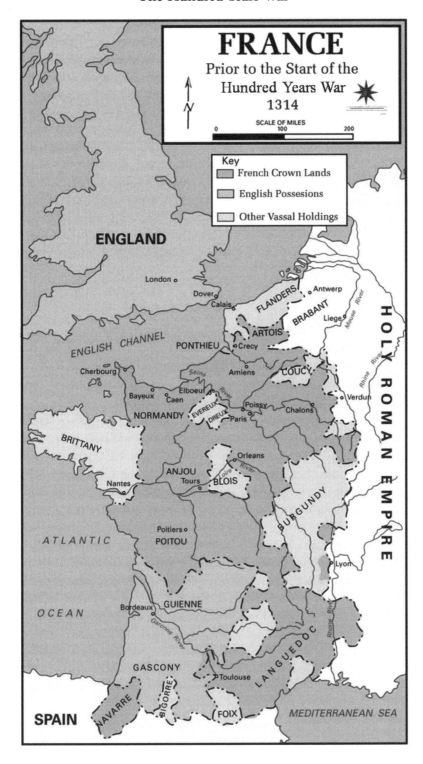

cousin, Philip Valois. The vast majority of the French nobility did not want to invite the 15-year-old king, the product of so much unrest in England, Scotland and Gascony, to be their new monarch. Not only was he their kingdom's greatest foreign rival, but his father Edward II, had proven himself a poor king, and England was currently under the regency of Isabella and her lover, Roger Mortimer. Instead, Philip received the crown and ushered in the Valois Dynasty. Edward was too young to yet contest Philip's claim, especially considering the tumultuous domestic politics he faced. It would be another ten years before he seriously challenged his rival's hold on the French throne.

Historians of the Hundred Years War generally subscribe to one of three schools of thought regarding the cause of the war.[6] The *feudal school*, perhaps the most popular, contends that Edward went to war with Philip to gain full suzerainty of his Gascon holdings in southern France. For them, any pretension Edward had for the French crown was mere jockeying for a stronger claim to an independent Gascony. By this line of reasoning, Edward's strategy was to assert his claim to the crown, embark upon a military campaign to bring Philip to the bargaining table, and then offer to abandon his claim to the entire kingdom in exchange for Philip's relinquishment of any feudal hold over Aquitaine, a dukedom that no one argued had been Edward's right to hold. Certainly one can acknowledge the reasonableness of this perspective. Events of 1346–1347 and 1355–1360 can surely be described to fit neatly into this interpretation, but there are other explanations for Edward's strategy.

The *dynastic school* supports the belief that Edward actually did believe in the validity of his claim to the French crown, and that he earnestly endeavoured to see it advanced. Its adherents often cite the technical validity of his claim by right through his mother, and also Edward's refusal of lesser terms when he was bargaining from the position of supreme power that accompanied the capture of King Jean II at Poitiers in 1356. Jean, in fact, offered not only a full renunciation of rights over Edward's hereditary lands in Aquitaine, but also granted very generous borders to those holdings by including additional adjacent territories.[7] If Edward's ultimate goal had been merely to wrest control of Aquitaine from the French king, then he accomplished these goals in the first twenty years of the war, and hostilities from his end, at least, would have ceased. But Edward continued the war for the rest of his life and generations of his successors, despite bankruptcy, plague and civil war, continued the struggle well into the next century. British sovereigns would not abandon the claim to the French throne, in fact, until Napoleon Bonaparte ruled the Continent and forced them to sign the Treaty of Amiens in 1802. There must have been some other factor that drove Edward to continue the war that was emptying his coffers and preventing him from securing his control of matters much closer to home.

The Hundred Years War

Those who subscribe to the third and perhaps least popular school, the *Scottish school*, offer a suggestion very closely related to politics internal to the British Isles. They propose that the key international dispute that drove Edward to war in the late 1330s was not directly associated with the French at all, but was rather a result of repeated Scottish incursions into the northern counties of England. His own kingdom's feeble response to these operations, which were backed by French support, both moral and monetary, had shamed Edward in his youth. Upon reaching the age of majority, he sought to right the wrongs that his countrymen and his own honour had suffered at the hands of the Scots, a people his grandfather, Edward I, 'Longshanks', had done so much to conquer. Edward I, much more martial than his father Henry III had been, had mobilized much of the kingdom's resources to unite the island under one ruler. England benefited not only from the expanded borders, but more from the bureaucratic and parliamentary reforms that had resulted. Edward III, upon taking the throne, would follow in the pattern of his distinguished grandfather, while having the added difficulty of needing to make up for all of the ground lost during the disastrous reign of Edward II.

Edward III found that opportunity to assert his claim to the French throne when Philip seized English lands in Aquitaine and Ponthieu on 24 May 1337. Philip accused Edward of violating his oath of fealty, and on this pretext exercised his prerogative as overlord of the Duchy of Aquitaine to claim direct rule of these holdings. The English king, as a minor, had been forced to pay homage to Charles twice, in 1329 and 1331. Edward responded to this latest demand with his only legal recourse, to denounce the legitimacy of Philip's hold on the French crown and assert himself as a more suitable sovereign. Not all French subjects immediately opposed the proposal. The Gascons largely favoured the English claim, not only because of their long-standing relationship with the English crown, but also because they viewed the proximity of a monarch in Paris as a much greater threat to their own autonomy than one separated from local affairs by the English Channel. Much of the relationship between England and Gascony centred on the latter's lucrative wine trade with the island kingdom. Similarly, France's northern neighbour, Flanders, also had strong financial ties with England, but in this instance because of the wool trade. The Flemings were famous for their textile production but relied heavily upon wool imported from the English countryside. Much like the Gascons, they also profited politically from a weak and divided France. The Flemings had taken oaths of fealty to the French king but Edward was able to circumvent this obstacle when he declared himself rightful heir to the French throne. While the pope considered the arguments made by each of the sovereigns' legal advocates, Edward and Philip postured for war.

Victory at Poitiers

Though most histories of the Hundred Years War focus upon the three great campaigns in which an English army invaded French soil, the second of which of course is the subject of this book, the war actually began in May of 1337 with French naval forces raiding English towns along the Channel coast. In 1339 Philip went so far as to assemble an invasion force of nearly 30,000 men, which historian Richard Barber has described as intending 'to repeat the Norman conquest of England'.[8] Edward responded by assuming the offensive. But despite his extensive planning, he failed to conduct an invasion of France in either 1337 or 1338. He had, during those years, however, managed to lay the groundwork for mobilizing his kingdom – its manpower, its wealth and its public will. By the autumn of 1339 Edward decided that he could wait no longer to act. He had assembled a force of sufficient size to alarm the French defenders, but his debts were mounting and he could not hope to indefinitely maintain his army – in particular, his foreign allies – if he delayed any longer.[9] The *chevauchée* that followed nearly led to a decisive battle being fought, but Philip changed his mind at the last moment and marched his army home to Paris. Perhaps one motivator for him to retire was his superstition, as recorded by the chronicler Froissart:

> In the midst of the debates of the council of the king of France, letters were brought to the king from Robert king of Sicily, addressed to him and his council. This king Robert was, as they said, a very great astrologer and full of deep science, he had often cast the nativities of the kings of France and England, and had found, by his astrology and the influence of the stars, that, if the king of France fought with the king of England in person, he would surely be defeated; in consequence of which he, as a wise king, and much fearing the danger and peril of his cousin the king of France, had sent long before letters, most earnestly to request king Philip and his council never to give battle to the English when king Edward should be there in person. These doubts, and this letter from the king of Sicily, made many of the lords of France sore disheartened, of which the king was informed, who, notwithstanding, was very eager for combat; but he was so strongly dissuaded from it, that the day passed quietly, and each man retired to his quarters.[10]

The campaign brought little benefit to either king, as Edward had emptied his coffers by for so long pursuing battle and Philip had forfeited his honour by avoiding it. In the end the Fabian-like strategy that the French king employed succeeded in foiling his rival's incursions, but they could not be employed forever, as they eroded his subjects' confidence in him as their protector. This perspective is most obvious in the words of Philip de Mézières, writing in the mid-fourteenth century:

The Hundred Years War

The ancient way of government of this kingdom has been badly interrupted and neglected. You can see the effects of this. Because of the taxes and the widespread devastation resulting from feeble defence, your people begin to complain and to say that they have been more harassed than free men should be. From such oppression are born treason and rebellion. Your royal councillors and great officers, on the other hand, complain that your subjects are not fulfilling their obligations. Thus there is no longer union between yourself and your people and this, in turn, has helped towards defeat in war.[11]

Edward seized on the one aspect of political success that he could claim to have gained in the campaign, and in January 1340 assumed the title of king of England and France. On 24 June of the same year, serving as his kingdom's foremost admiral as well as general, he defeated the French invasion force at the battle of Sluys, a battle which can only be compared in strategic significance to Nelson's victory several centuries later at Trafalgar, which would once again dash French hopes of storming English beaches. The battle, in fact, can be considered the progenitor of the English strategic reliance on naval defence of the Channel.[12] Edward retook the offensive, and by the end of July was gathering a large force outside the walls of Tournai.

After two months of posturing in an attempt to bring Philip to battle by the threat of a full-scale siege, the two monarchs signed the Truce of Esplechin on 25 September. Philip would not fight and Edward could not delay; he had no means to pay his army. In these two engagements, the French king showed tremendous resiliency. The defeat at Sluys had been a blow to his prestige and a critical impediment to his strategic options. Not only had several thousand soldiers died, but the loss of his fleet forced him to resume the defensive. In this way it was a defining moment in determining the character of the war for the next 113 years. Tournai had taught each rival king a different lesson. Edward learned that he had to revamp his finances before making another attempt at a settlement of the conflict by feat of arms. It would take more than a siege to draw Philip into battle, and Edward was becoming increasingly convinced that a single decisive battle was his surest path to ultimate victory. Philip learned that Edward's reputed tactical prowess was offset by his lack of operational stamina. Neither his war chest nor his allies could sustain a prolonged contest. The question that remained was how long Philip's honour could withstand this winning strategy.

One must wonder whether Philip compared himself to Quintus Fabius Maximus, the famed commander whom Plutarch tells us had been dubbed the 'shield of Rome' for defending the great city from Hannibal Barca. In truth, the Second Punic War possesses a number of similarities with the Hundred Years

Victory at Poitiers

War in that the aggressor (Hannibal) won three great victories over the defenders, the latter having a wealthier and more extensive empire.[13] Additionally, Philip's avoidance strategies can undoubtedly be classified as *Fabian* and proved just as effective. Each despot's refusal to engage in direct combat while his lands were ravaged resulted in so much criticism by their subordinates that the French king should have considered himself very fortunate that he did not have Fabius' cognomen 'cunctator' bestowed upon him.

Hostilities between England and France reopened a year and a half later with, of course, another succession controversy, this time in Brittany. The peninsular dukedom was at this time still independent, and its resources and size made it desirable, if only as an ally, to both kings. The civil unrest that resulted could effectively be described as a proxy war between Edward and Philip. Edward supported as successor to the title John de Montfort, the late Duke's half-brother. Philip lent his aid to Jeanne de Flandre, a niece married to Charles of Blois, a famous commander and trusted vassal of the French king. Opposed by Philip, John assumed the operational offensive and seized the majority of the contested lands in only two months during the summer of 1341. Edward took advantage of the distraction to expand his holdings in Gascony. Philip concentrated instead in the north, and sent Charles and a Norman army to retake Brittany – an endeavour in which they proved very successful. John fell into the hands of the French king, leaving his countess to carry on the war in his stead. Late the next spring Edward sent one of his most capable commanders, Walter de Mauny, to assist. That summer, the Earl of Northampton also arrived on the Continent, at the head of a small army.

On 30 September 1342, at the battle of Morlaix, Northampton defeated a French force under Charles of Blois that outnumbered the English army perhaps four to one, but the victory was incomplete and the battle indecisive because Northampton could not or would not pursue Blois' retreating forces.[14] Four weeks later Edward arrived on the Continent and prepared to battle Philip. Robert of Artois had been besieging the French town of Vannes when Edward arrived, but was mortally wounded outside its walls.[15] A month later Philip brought his army to relieve the town, but, though he formed them for battle, there was to be no fighting. Instead the parties signed the Treaty of Malestroit. The treaty effectively called for a three-year ceasefire, with each king retaining the cities and lands he had held at the time of the signing. The matter of the succession of Brittany was not so easily settled; the contest continued until 1364.

The Lessons of Crécy

In April of 1345, Gascon nobles requested military aid to help defend their borders from not only royal French incursions, but also those of the Count de l'Isle, whom Froissart reports 'was at that time like a king in Gascony, and had been so since the commencement of the wars between the two Kings. He had taken the field, captured towns and castles, and waged war upon all who were of the English party.'[16] To combat this threat and at the same time strengthen the loyalties of his Continental vassals, King Edward III sent his most trusted general, Henry of Lancaster, the Earl of Derby, to Bordeaux with 500 men-at-arms and 1,000 longbowmen. Among the host were some very distinguished knights of the day, including the Earl of Pembroke, the Earl of Oxford, the Lord Stafford, Sir Walter Mauny and Sir Frank van Halle. The king knew that open hostilities left unchecked would undermine royal authority in the area. It was an issue he contended with regularly on the border with Scotland, and was a fact of war that he was depending upon as the foundation of his strategy against Philip.

At the same time as Lancaster sought to reassert his English lord's authority in the south by beginning with an attack against the rebellious nobles who were rapidly assembling against him at Bergerac, Edward III sent the Earl of Northampton to Brittany with a smaller force. The king himself was to land in Normandy with the bulk of the army. Together, they would threaten Philip from all sides. Several chroniclers, including Froissart, report that the English king's original objective was to join Lancaster in Gascony, particularly since Philip had sent a large force under his eldest son, Jean, the Duke of Normandy, to confront the English commander who had been enjoying so much success. Lancaster, now Earl of Lancaster in addition to Derby, since his father had recently died and passed to him the title, had consolidated his forces at Aiguillon, between Bordeaux and Toulouse, and had fortified the town. His preparations were well-timed, for they enabled him to withstand Jean's siege, which would last into the following summer.

Unfavourable winds and the counsel of Godfrey d'Harcourt are alternately cited as the chief reasons for Edward's changes in destination. Bartholomew Burghersh is most vocal on the matter. He writes that King Edward was intending to go to Gascony [...] but the wind was so adverse that he could not hold to this course at all [...] Since it did not please God that he should go in that direction, he decided to land wherever God should give him grace to do so, and thus arrived well and in good heart with all the fleet in the part of Normandy called the Cotentin.'[17]

The *Acts of War* also mention the poor weather, but suggest that when the long delay ended, 'our Lord helped the king of England, and the winds and tide were favourable', and the king landed safely on the Cotentin. There is no mention made of an intention for any other previous destination.[18] Le Bel, to the contrary, reports that Edward had 'good fortune at sea'.[19] Froissart credits Godfrey d'Harcourt, a disenfranchised Norman, with instigating the change in destination.[20] The *Grandes Chronique* blames d'Harcourt for the devastation of the Cotentin, but not for its selection.[21] Both the *Scalachronica* and Chandos' Herald are silent on the matter.[22] Whatever the cause, the English army landed in St Vaast-la-Hougue, 20 miles east of Cherbourg, on 12 July 1346. From there Edward began what would become his most decisive, and most historically contentious, military campaign.

Few key aspects of the campaign are free from debate, but the most critical discourse centres on Edward's strategic and operational goals. This argument, significantly, has implications for questions larger than the purpose of one mid-fourteenth-century invasion: it helps us understand the workings of medieval military thought. Edward's lieutenant in the south had experienced tremendous success but now his campaign had stalled. The king needed to reinforce Lancaster but recognized this could be accomplished better by indirect means. Had the king sailed to Bordeaux, where he undoubtedly would have been able to rally additional troops under his banner, he would have left a crossing of the English Channel uncontested. By instead initiating a campaign into Normandy, he at once relieved Lancaster's besieged army, threatened the French capital, reoccupied his hereditary holdings, and did all this while occupying a position that blocked any invasion of his own kingdom. The *Grandes Chronique* reports that such danger did exist, for 'in this year, the king of France proposed to prepare a great armada of ships to cross over to England', but his fleet was not yet ready when Edward pre-emptively struck.[23]

Most historians agree that Edward III had entered Normandy in the summer of 1346 to either reassert his hereditary claims in the region, or, more likely, to cut a swath of devastation across the countryside of France, feeding his army on pillage and plunder. What would the purpose of this campaign of rapine be? If it was to humble Philip and convince his subjects that he could not protect them from the ravages of the English claimant to the throne, then that Edward certainly accomplished. But would such activity bring Edward any closer to the throne? Who was worse to have as your king: one who could not defend your land from ruin, or the inflictor of destruction himself? On this point historians claim that the English king repeatedly ordered his army not to molest the townspeople who surrendered to the invaders and swore fealty, but that these orders were almost entirely ignored, and Edward made no drastic changes in his conduct of the operation to prevent their reoccurrence. The primary sources do not bear this out, however. According to le Bel, as soon as the English landed, Edward 'sent a third of his men to burn and waste the coastal lands'.[24] Even if the king had not ordered the pillaging, he certainly collected his share of the gains, because 'with it King Edward was able to pay his soldiers generously'.[25] The chronicler, Henry Knighton, writes that Edward 'captured the towns of La Hogue and Barfleur and did with them what he would'.[26] Chandos' Herald speaks more of the prince's role, reporting that 'All the Cotentin he overrode and wholly burnt and laid waste.'[27] The attendant clergy who provided accounts were more benign in their description of events but that is to be expected. Northburgh is even apologetic, writing that when the English sacked Carentan, 'a lot of wine and food was found there, and much of the town was burnt, the king being unable to prevent it'.[28] This leads us to a debate among historians who argue over to what extent King Edward truly sought to prevent or at least minimize his troops' despoilment of the Cotentin. In what has been termed the 'La Hogue proclamation', Edward may have forbidden the widespread devastation. Whether he was successful in restraining his men is another question altogether. Scholar and Crécy expert, Andrew Ayton, discusses the merits of the various arguments in his examination of the campaign, concluding that the English king most likely protected Norman holdings loyal to the English crown, but that much of the rest of the peninsula suffered horribly as the invaders journeyed east towards Paris.[29]

If one argues that Edward was not truly pursuing the French crown, the *chevauchée* could be viewed as a mere raid by which he could enrich his own army while inflicting harm to his enemy's reputation and tax base. It could also serve as a warning for Philip to cease meddling in Scottish affairs. But one must not be tempted to view Edward's ride through Normandy independently of his concurrent operations. It must be remembered that there were other English and allied armies operating in France. At the very least, one could suggest that the *chevauchée* was designed to relieve the besieged forces under Lancaster at Aiguillon. Even this does not sufficiently account for Edward's strategy, however, because he had conceived of the multi-pronged invasion long before Lancaster had found himself in his current predicament.

Motive is no easier for a historian to prove than it is for a criminal lawyer. It is one thing to demonstrate where and when an army manoeuvred, it is quite another to prove beyond question why the commander made the decisions he did. When assessing Edward's strategy for the 1346 campaign we have many sources on which to base our judgment. Each, however, has its flaws. Chronicles – even those written by eyewitnesses – were necessarily written only after the events they record, and often at the bequest of the victor. That they name Calais as Edward's ultimate objective can be easily discounted as the product of hindsight. The natural solution to this then would appear to be reliance upon dispatches issued during the campaign itself. These, however, have also been discredited because of their obvious value as tools of propaganda. Counter to the generally accepted views by other historians, Rogers presents a convincing argument in his *War Cruel and Sharp*, which bears recapitulation here. But perhaps it is best to view events as they occurred before making any pronouncement regarding the strategy that drove them.

Edward III had brought with him over 15,000 men – 90 per cent of the English troops deployed in support of the three-pronged invasion. Edward had with him 2,800 men-at-arms, 2,500 Welsh spearmen, 3,000 mounted archers, and 7,000 longbowmen. Many great names will be recognized among the knights who accompanied him on the invasion: the 16-year-old Prince Edward, the Earls of Hereford, Northampton, Arundel, Cornwall, Warwick, Huntingdon, Suffolk, Oxford, the Lord of Mowbray, John Chandos, Peter and James Audley, and Bartholomew of Burghersh, as well as numerous others, including some Flemish and German nobles. Edward's first act, according to many sources, was to knight some of the younger nobles in his army, including Prince Edward, Sir Roger Mortimer and Sir William Montagu.[30] The young prince would, when in command of his own army in Spain two decades later, repeat this act, knighting many among his host when battle was imminent.[31] Froissart includes an amusing anecdote that may have had some basis in fact, but was probably included to reinforce chivalric notions of magnanimity and divine purpose:

> When the fleet of England was all safely arrived at La Hogue, the king leaped on shore first; but by accident he fell, and with such violence that the blood gushed out at his nose: the knights that were near him said, 'Dear sir, let us entreat you to return to your ship, and not think of landing today, for this is an unfortunate omen.' The king instantly replied, 'For why? I look upon it as very favourable, and a sign that the land is desirous of me.' His people were much pleased with his answer.[32]

Edward spent six days in the port town, presumably to organize his forces, reconnoitre his intended route, and continue to develop his plan of action. It seems reasonable that he would want to weigh the Normans' reaction to his arrival. He used his maritime forces to exact the submission of Barfleur, a port town approximately 5 miles north of his landing site, as well as Cherbourg, another good port at the tip of the Cotentin, and Montebourg. After nearly a week at St Vaast-la-Hougue, the march got underway. The English army headed toward the great cities of Normandy – Caen and Rouen, which lay on the road to the French capital. Sir Godfrey d'Harcourt, whom the chronicler Jean le Bel reports had recently fallen from Philip's favour, had advised Edward during the voyage that, 'the country of Normandy is one of the plenteous countries of the world: sir, on jeopardy of my head, if ye will land there, there is none that shall resist you; the people of Normandy have not been used to the War, and all the knights and squires of the country are now at the siege before Aiguillon with the Duke'. This assurance of an invasion route free of armed resistance was mirrored by Philip to his Scottish allies at virtually the same moment, when he promised that none of Edward's soldiers would be present to defend the north of England because they were busy on campaign in France.

Philip, unsure of where Edward would land, had spread his forces throughout the region, but had nowhere left sufficient men to mount any sort of resistance. Edward had brought with him an imposing army and this, coupled with the torn loyalties of the Normans, greatly reduced the chance of them mounting a defiant defence. Those men who did choose to support the French king, being of such a minority, necessarily holed themselves up in fortifications. Edward, however, showed little interest in reducing these pockets of resistance. The countryside was rich in foodstuffs and plunder and time was short. The English had the advantage in numbers for the time being but the situation could not be expected to last. Edward took advantage of the current state of affairs and spread his forces into three divisions that marched abreast to maximize the amount of land they could pillage. He appointed Godfrey d'Harcourt and the Earl of Warwick as marshals in command of his left and right flanking divisions, respectively. The Earl of Arundel was his constable. The prince rode with his father in the centre division. Froissart reports that the timing for an invasion was excellent: the larders were full and the English army could effectively live off of the land without being tied to logistical trains. The three divisions marched separately during the day but reunited every evening to camp in security. The march to Caen, the first great city of Normandy that they would encounter, took the invaders eight days to complete. Along the way they passed through several towns without resistance, though the townspeople did show defiance by breaking bridges to slow the English advance. In this way the towns of Valognes, Carentan, St Lo, Sept Vents, Torteval and Fontenay found themselves unwilling provisioners for Edward's army, which quickly earned a reputation for unbridled violence.

Despite le Bel's damning judgments that 'he allowed various parts of his kingdom to be laid waste and pillaged while he remained in or around Paris for an easy life and his own safety', Philip was not inactive during this period, though he yet made no move against this threat to his kingdom. Having recently dispatched a large army to Gascony to counter Lancaster's advances there, Philip undoubtedly had at least a little difficulty in raising additional forces. But the French king had many allies and an even greater number of vassals, and fear of the chaos caused by Edward's approaching devastation certainly encouraged some nobles to not only support the French king but to urge him to take up arms against the invader. Though loss of property and life were prime motivators in their call to arms, one cannot discount the role that honour played in affecting one's decision to go to war. Philip's land had been invaded in the south and his vassals there disgraced by their collective inability to resist. The new threat in the north, however, was led by a challenger to his throne and Philip was in increasing danger of losing to Edward not only the lands of the old Angevin empire, but also the confidence of those by which he maintained his hold on the realm.

By 25 July, after a full week on the march, the English army camped at Fontenay, just 10 miles from Caen. At some point along the march, possibly when the initial phase of raids was over and the army departed la Hogue, Prince Edward assumed command of the vanguard. He held this position of honour ably assisted by the earls of Northampton and Warwick. Caen, situated on the Orne river, was the first sizeable town that Edward would encounter, and he probably expected the French to make a defensive stand to prevent its fall. The young prince would have welcomed such a meeting. Edward had been avoiding

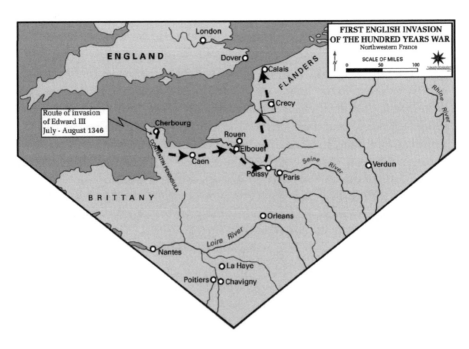

falling prey to strategic consumption, the process by which an army's numbers attrit due to subordinate manning requirements, such as garrison duty. He accomplished this by garrisoning his newly-claimed towns with local supporters rather than any of the soldiers he had brought with him across the Channel – these he was conserving for the inevitable confrontation with Philip.

Caen consisted of an old and a new section. The former had an adjacent castle, much of which had been built by Edward's ancestors when England had a firmer hold on Normandy. The new town was built on an island between the Orne and a loop formed by one of its subsidiary branches. Thus surrounded on all sides by water, the new town was inaccessible except by its three bridges, each of which was heavily fortified. Not far from the western wall of the old town was an abbey reputed to hold the remains of William the Conqueror. This, of course, would have been a point of interest for the English king, enacting his ancestor's invasion in reverse. Approximately the same distance in the opposite direction from the eastern wall of the town was another abbey, this one housing the remains of the venerable English queen, Matilda. Edward demonstrated that he expected a fight at this point in his advance by abandoning his practice of marching along parallel routes, and instead consolidating his men into a single column. He had sent forward scouting parties and had received word that the Bishop of Bayeux had assumed command of the defence of the castle and that the constable of France, the Count of Eu, was present in the town, preparing its defence.

The English attack began with an assault against one of the bridges, led by Warwick. It encountered determined resistance at first, and Bartholomew de Burghersh attributed the initial lack of success to the fact that Warwick's contingent was wholly made up of archers. Whatever its composition, Warwick's men were able to break through when the defenders began retreating. The Normans had learned that an attack against one of the other bridges had been successful, and sought to find asylum in the castle with the bishop's men. Some Welsh soldiers, likely among those raised by Prince Edward, the Prince of Wales, had found a fordable crossing site that had allowed them to circumvent the fortifications guarding each bridge. The Earl of Northampton and Sir John Talbot brought troops to reinforce Warwick's success. More steadfast than the majority of his soldiers, the constable and Chamberlain de Tancarville defended the bridge despite being abandoned there, and were taken prisoner by Sir Thomas Holland, a member of the prince's retinue. Part of King Edward's fleet had found the mouth of the Orne and sailed up it to Caen's harbour. It defeated the few ships there and provided small boats to shuttle men across the narrow river to the now-unprotected town. English soldiers thus advanced from all sides and made the citizens of Caen pay for having dared to attempt a defence. Sources report more than 2,500 killed in the mêlée. The *Acta Bellicosa* of Edward

III reports that the bishop was able to hold out for one more day in the old castle, but that on the 27th he surrendered to his besieger.

The victorious king spent four more days at Caen, permitting his men to plunder the town and countryside, though he gave orders to safeguard the lives of the local populace. Bartholomew de Burghersh, who apparently was Edward's vanguard commander of choice, used these few days to lay waste the surrounding region, gaining provisions for the invasion force and burning everything else, particularly Philip's residences in the area. Edward used his fleet to unburden himself of the booty accumulated, which included jewels and much cloth – Caen was well known for its cloth industry – but the most profit was gained from the ransom of the scores of prisoners captured in the town. Hundreds of English ships took all this precious cargo back across the Channel. Fifteen nobles of Bayeux, not desiring to share Caen's fate, arrived to offer their surrender and a generous payment of protection money. Edward dismissed them out of hand. He did not want the burden of garrisoning another city now. He needed all available manpower for the fight he anticipated would not be long in coming.

Hearing that Philip was preparing to defend at Rouen, the Norman capital, only 60 miles further to the east, Edward took advantage of this brief rest to prepare for the next phase of the campaign, which he believed would involve a major battle with his rival at the head of a formidable army. His preparations included a requisition sent to London in the hands of a very ill William, Earl of Huntingdon, on 29 July for additional money, bows, bowstrings, and arrows. These the English king requested to be brought by ship from England to the port of Le Crotoy at the mouth of the Somme, more than 100 miles north of Paris. Clearly Edward anticipated not only a great march that would necessarily cross the Seine, pass Rouen (where he knew Philip to be) and come within a few days' march of Paris, but he wanted to be able to continue the invasion. This necessitated money for pay, for as he wrote in the request, 'although many of our people have been comforted by the profit they have made, we ourselves have gained nothing, but the whole burden rests on us, and our people press us much for their wages'.[33] War-making was expensive business and even this *chevauchée*, perhaps the most lucrative of the forms of war, was not self-sustaining. The other specific request was for materials and equipment to refit his great tactical advantage over Philip: his longbowmen.

Edward marched through the towns of Troarne and Rumesnil before arriving at Lisieux on the River Touques. There the English were greeted by papal emissaries who offered little in exchange for peace: Edward would have his ducal lands of Aquitaine restored to him. Philip had arrived with his army at Rouen that same day, 2 August. Edward continued his march unabated to the Seine. He stopped his eastward progress five days later when he was 12 miles south-west of Rouen at Elbeuf. Philip at this point withdrew his army to Paris, where he was assembling even more men. Now barely 60 miles north-west of the capital, Edward began walking up the south bank of the Seine, seeking a point at which to cross. Neither army wished to weaken its own position by being the one to traverse the obstacle, particularly with the other army waiting on the far shore. The river would then be at the crosser's back, making him even more vulnerable without an escape route or room to manoeuvre or forage. But Philip appeared to be in no rush to face Edward in battle. He destroyed most of the bridges along the Seine, drawing Edward ever nearer to Paris. The English finally forced a crossing at Poissy, thanks in large part to the daring of Northampton. Once on the north bank of the Seine, Edward found that he had no need to fear an attack by the French army. In fact, he could not coax them into a battle. He wrote a taunting letter to Philip from his headquarters at Auteuil on 17 August, ending it with a clear challenge:

> let it be known that at whatever hour you approach you will find us ready to meet you in the field, with God's help, which thing we most earnestly desire for the common good of Christendom, since you will not accept or offer any reasonable terms for peace.[34]

'Reasonable', to Edward, meant full suzerainty over Aquitaine. He would not have accepted less, and he could not hope that Philip would offer that which the English king for six years had professed to claim: the crown of France.

Philip did not accept Edward's challenge, nor did he offer new terms of peace. He did, however, offer to fight a pitched battle on the plains south of Paris. There, the Valois king would be able to field perhaps as many as 60,000 soldiers on ground of his own choosing. Edward was not foolish enough to accept battle on those terms. He sent the prince's division to ravage the outskirts of Paris, and then turned north, heading for Calais. It must be remembered that the English king had directed a few weeks before that money and supplies for his archers be sent to a port at the mouth of the Somme. But Jean le Bel indicates that Edward had additional strategic reasons for redirecting his campaign at this point. He writes that 'his chief intention was to lay siege to the strong town of Calais, since he could not entice King Phillippe to battle as he wished'.

As Edward marched north, his divisions fanned out into the countryside between the Seine and the Somme to despoil as much of it as they could. They continued to collect booty, which must have kept morale high for the soldiers, but also for the commanders, and especially Edward III, who was experiencing his typical fiscal shortages. The raids, as would be expected, had an equally disheartening effect on their victims. Philip, who had been gathering his forces at St Denis, realized that Edward would not attack him where he had wished, so he pursued the English king, presuming to force a battle near Amiens, 80 miles to the north. Passing through the territory so closely behind his adversary, Philip would have seen first-hand the devastation his subjects had suffered. As he became incensed, so, too, would his knights become more eager for battle. It was a tremendous breach of their honour that they should allow a force so much their numerical inferior to treat Philip's royal authority with such contempt. Their eagerness would prove their undoing when they finally caught up with the English army on the fields outside Crécy. But first the two armies would have to cross the Somme.

Consistent with the air of divine sanction that Edward possessed throughout the campaign, his Somme crossing was such that many would interpret it as evidence of God's support of the English invasion.[35] Since Philip had ordered the destruction of all the bridges the English army might have used to cross the Somme, Edward had to continue north along the southern bank until he found a suitable ford. John Capgrave's description of the event is reminiscent of the great fortune the Black Prince and Warwick would later experience when fording the Miosson at Poitiers: 'Than went thei [they] over the water of Summe, and fond [found] a passage that was nevir founde before.'[36] Edward had discovered among the recent captives, Gobin Agace, a local man with English sympathies – or at least without sufficient loyalty to the French king to forego enabling Edward to continue his campaign. Gobin Agace described to the English king 'where he and his whole army may pass the river Somme without any risk'.[37] He continued:

> There are certain fordable places where you may pass twelve men abreast twice in the day, and not have the water above your knees; but when the tide is in, the river is full and deep, and no one can cross it; when the tide is out, the river is so low that it may be passed, on horseback or on foot, without danger. The bottom of this ford is very hard, of gravel and white stones, over which all your carriages may safely pass, and from thence is called Blanchetaque.[38]

This information provided a tremendous boon for Edward, who otherwise may not have been able to cross the river at all. He rewarded the guide with a large cash gift.[39] The tidal ford described by Gobin Agace was not unknown to the local defenders, however, and when Edward's army arrived there at sunrise they were met by a blocking force that would complicate the crossing.[40]

The sources vary on the width of the crossing. While Froissart, as seen above, suggested a fairly narrow ford, Knighton reports that it was 'about a league wide',[41] and Chandos' Herald writes that 100 English knights 'with one accord dashed into the water on their chargers, lance couched'.[42] Edward himself reported that his men 'crossed a thousand people abreast […] in a single hour'.[43] A wide ford is likely, as on the other side Sir Godemar du Fay had formed up his several thousand defenders. Knighton reports that the opposing French forces numbered 3,000 and were under 'the commanders of Ponthieu and the Countess of Aumarle'.[44] Froissart names Godemar as the specific commander, and writes that he led 1,000 men-at-arms, 12,000 other soldiers, and a contingent of Genoese mercenaries armed with crossbows.[45] Historians have accepted more modest numbers, perhaps 500 men-at-arms and 3,000 other soldiers, including the Genoese crossbowmen.[46] This would be the French soldiers' first taste of massed longbow fire. The Prince of Wales (he would not be called the Black Prince until after Crécy) ordered the vanguard to attack. The English archers fired and 100 knights with couched lances charged across the shallow water. The assault proved too much for Godemar's defenders, who were largely untrained and poorly armed townspeople. The chroniclers report up to 2,000 French casualties, the vast majority of whom would have come from among the unmounted contingent.[47] Within an hour the last of Edward's army had crossed. The knights engaged in a brief pursuit, but quickly reconsolidated just as Philip's army reached the south bank of the river.[48] The French king, himself, was still in Abbeville. Edward kept his army on the opposite bank for more than a day, daring the French to attempt to force a river crossing. Rather than partaking in such a foolish endeavour, Philip's army returned to Abbeville. Once satisfied that the French could not cross at the same ford, Edward marched his army through the Crécy wood and prepared for battle.

'King Edward, passing the forest of Cressy, was sodenly beset with Philip Valoys great hoste: but he chase a plot of ground equal to fight yn, and wan a great victory of hym.'[49] With these words Sir Thomas Gray, author of the *Scalachronica*, described the climax of Edward III's 1346 *chevauchée*. The Scottish chronicler did not assign responsibility for the English victory to Edward's valour, Philip's blunders, or even God's favour. He ascribed singular importance to the ground on which the English king had chosen to fight. This site, therefore, deserves our attention.

Whether the French army approached the English along one route or several, we do know that it spent the previous night in Abbeville. The lead cavalry units were the first to reach the battlefield, followed by some Genoese crossbowmen. All were in a rush to reassert their honour, which they felt had been tarnished by Philip's reluctance to face Edward in battle. The French king was probably still a good distance from the English when the invaders' formation was sighted. The French dismounted infantry were surely far behind their faster-moving compatriots. Philip had delayed this battle for so long because he was waiting until he could assemble such a force as to dwarf the English invaders, thus assuring

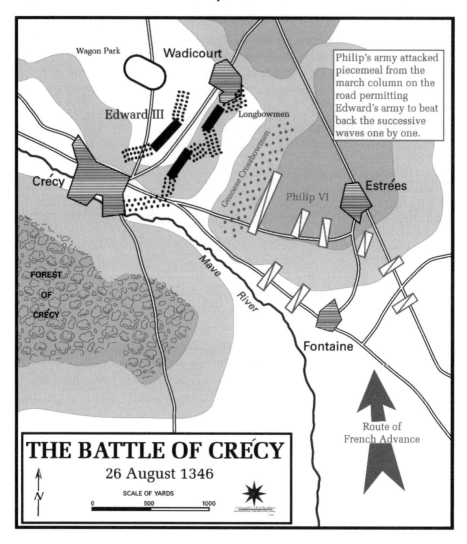

Philip's army attacked piecemeal from the march column on the road permitting Edward's army to beat back the successive waves one by one.

THE BATTLE OF CRÉCY

26 August 1346

SCALE OF YARDS

0   500   1000

Route of French Advance

victory. By the time he left Paris he had amassed 40,000 men – nearly three times the number in the English army. Now he risked losing his tremendous advantage in numbers by attacking piecemeal. To prevent such a tactical misstep, he issued orders for the vanguard to wait for the rest of his host to arrive from Abbeville. The haughty knights at the head of the formation, however, each wanted the honour of striking the first blow against the English assembled before them, and would not heed his commands. Even when they waited for the crossbowmen to advance, they did not pause long enough to permit the mercenary archers time to retrieve their shields from the baggage, further back in the trains. This would prove one of many fateful decisions made that day.

The Lessons of Crécy

Historians generally accept the French line of advance to have been roughly along modern route D 56, indicated by the solid arrow on the accompanying map. The 16-mile march from Abbeville would have left them wanting for water, which they would seek to replenish in the streams marked by Box 1 (see map on p. 38). Some historians have depicted the French advancing along multiple lines, one possibility being marked by the dashed arrow. However, the point is irrelevant to a discussion of the actual attack against the English position, because the terrain, particularly the steep bank in Box 2, would have funnelled them back to the west to attack around the left side of the wood, Box 3. Were they to have attacked midway between the two villages, as is often proposed, they would have been forced to descend the bank at a height of 4 to 5 metres. Even there, it was completely impassable for any cavalry formation, and further north along the bank increases in height to 7 metres.

Taking into account the state of mind of the knights of the French vanguard – their eagerness for battle is well documented – it seems likely that they would have endeavoured to strike at the English lines where they saw them arrayed. The French were in no mood for sophisticated turning manoeuvres. Certainly no primary source, nor any historian since, contends that the French attempted anything other than a direct frontal assault. Thus, the location of the attack can best be determined by examining the disposition of the English defence.

A trip to the historic battlefield, with the requisite visit to the new but growing local museum, would yield no definitive answer regarding the tactical defence that King Edward devised on that day six and a half centuries ago. There are no fewer than four different possibilities depicted in sketches by various historians. Yet another, heretofore unexamined possibility must be considered. The sources report that the English king arrayed his forces between the villages of Crécy-en-Ponthieu and Wadicourt, and most historians have taken this description very literally. The two villages were over 1,500 metres apart. Had Edward set his men in a solid line stretching from one village to the other, the 2,400 men-at-arms he had committed to the lead divisions could have averaged a depth of only one to two ranks. This would in no way have been feasible for any sort of defence. Even if the 2,500 Welsh spearmen were included in the line, as they most certainly were in some way, the ranks would have been only three men deep. English armies of the period typically fought with ranks at least six men deep. Certainly a depth of only three men would not have withstood the fifteen heavy cavalry charges that the French were to make that day. Of course, Edward did have 7,000 archers in his army. We must not underestimate them the way that Philip did. If they took up positions forming wings on either end of the formations of men-at-arms, the combined 12,000 soldiers could have formed a block of men eight ranks deep spanning the entire distance. Clearly Edward's remaining 400 men-at-arms and 3,000 mounted archers would not take up position in this line, as the sources agree that he kept these in reserve. A solid line of 12,000 is not a feasible solution, however, for several reasons. First, the Black Prince's division, which assumed the place of honour on the English right flank, did most of the fighting at Crécy. It seems implausible that so many men would maintain equal spacing and distribution for the several hours that the battle lasted, when only one end of the formation was being attacked. And yet we know how many men and of what type each division of the English army had. And Edward III's famous denial of reinforcements to his son when the fighting was at its hottest should dissuade any from suggesting that there was a mass reallocation of troops occurring during the battle.

A second point to consider is the effective range of the longbow. In order for the 12,000 men to stretch the full distance between the two villages with a depth of eight ranks, they would had to have maintained a straight line. Sources indicate, however, that the wings of longbowmen extended forward at an angle, so that a certain amount of crossfire existed to the front of the men-at-arms.[50] The battlefield lends itself to such a disposition, as a natural ridgeline creates a bowl in which it is believed most French casualties were taken. Historian Jim Bradbury examines the chroniclers' descriptions of the disposition of the archers and uses them to derive several conclusions about their arrangement at Crécy and other battles of the Hundred Years War. After challenging the seemingly widely held belief that archers were employed according to a strict template throughout the conflict, he reassesses Froissart's use of the enigmatic term 'herce' to describe the shape of the archers' formation. He suggests that it may have been a comparison to a hedgehog.[51] This explanation would fit neatly with our diagram if one considers the bristles of the Welsh spearmen backed by the points of arrows directed towards the enemy. Historian Michael Prestwich describes another explanation for the chronicler's enigmatic choice of words: 'a harrow-shaped triangular frame, designed to carry candles [...] in Holy Week'.[52] But how exactly were the archers arranged in a triangle? The formation I propose here satisfies both the triangular aspect of the 'herce' and the suggestion that other chroniclers put forward that the longbowmen formed wings on either end of the infantry. Rogers' use of the *Chronicle of St Omer* does not have to contradict this proposal, either.[53] The three battles are present, the Black Prince's van on the right, the second division under the Earls of Northampton and Arundel on the left, and King Edward's to the rear. The archers flank the men-at-arms, and form a triangular projection. This interpretation could also fit with Bradbury's proposal that the archers formed a 'forward flanking position'.[54] The unsupported archers that he describes could easily be those positioned at right angles on the far extremities, whose mission was to refuse the flank. Although Rogers argues that the divisions may have been arranged in column, the configuration proposed here follows much of the same logic, with the Black Prince's division doing the vast majority of the fighting, the king's division to the rear with a better vantage from which to command the battle, and archers flanking the primary divisions of men-at-arms.[55] Prestwich, though favouring Rogers' columnar formation, agrees that they would have been 'concentrated towards the southern end of the ridge'.[56] This interpretation coincides well with Froissart's description of their array:

> [The Prince's] archers were formed in the manner of a portcullis, or harrow, and the men-at-arms in the rear. The earls of Northampton and Arundel, who commanded the second division, had posted themselves in good order on his wing, to assist and succour the prince, if necessary.[57]

Le Baker also confirms the positioning, writing that 'The archers were also assigned a place apart from the men-at-arms, so that they were positioned at the sides of the army almost like wings; in this way they did not hinder the men-at-arms, nor did they meet the enemy head on, but could catch them in their crossfire.'[58]

In the following map the solid bars denote dismounted men-at-arms. The dotted lines represent archers. The solid square approximates the location of the windmill from which Edward III directed the battle. The archers would have been well-served tying into the terraces (1). They could have prepared to refuse any attempt against their right flank by having an additional line of archers, perhaps of 50 metres, angled along the edge of the terrace. Froissart perhaps alludes to this defensive arrangement when he tells us that 'The king of France was eager to march to the place where he saw their banners displayed, but there was a hedge of archers before him.'[59] The Black Prince's 1,200 men-at-arms occupied a line of approximately 150 metres. This would have allowed for a depth of eight ranks – appropriate considering the great proportion of fighting for which his battle would be responsible. The next two lines of archers (2) would have been able to take advantage of the sloped terrain by occupying a total of 700 metres. If 400 archers were detached to protect the baggage trains (2,000 would later be used as a reserve at the battle of Verneuil in 1424), the remaining 5,600 archers (including Northampton's 3,000) could be evenly distributed into eight ranks along the entire line. Likely, the stock of arrows would not have been evenly distributed but supplied in greatest proportion to the most active parts of the line.

Similarly, the prince's 3,000 Welsh spearmen could form four ranks along the whole front of the archers, at the bottom of the slope with the archers occupying the vantage position, perhaps with 200 concentrated at the weakest point in the line (3). The English far left (4) would reflect their efforts to refuse the right flank, and would fire directly into the great bank, which would be well

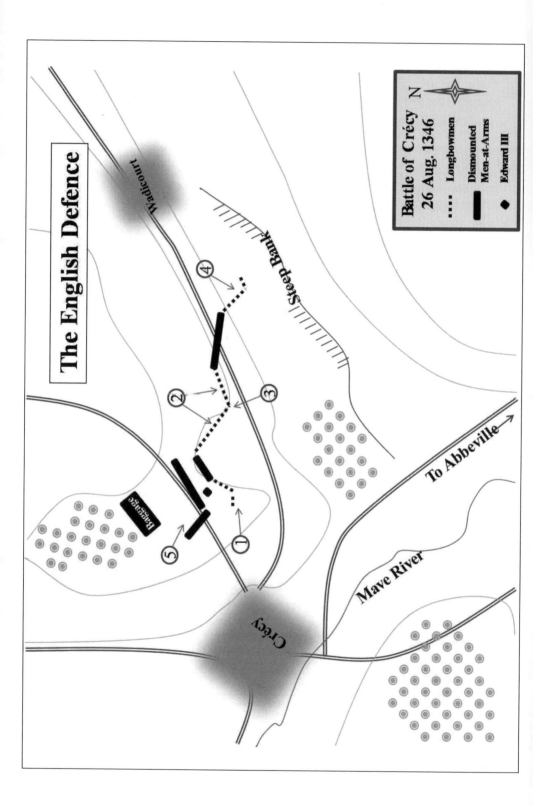

within their bowshot. Any French who attempted to advance through this valley to outflank the English right (as they would have to do if they did not want to circumnavigate all of Wadicourt), would suffer quickly for their underestimation of the power of the English longbow. King Edward's reserve of 1,600 men-at-arms and 4,000 archers (5), would have contributed to the fight in three key roles:

1) To prevent the French from outflanking the English far right by circumnavigating Crécy.
2) To protect the king (who was in or near the windmill).
3) To be prepared to fill gaps in the line.

This position accounts for all three of these responsibilities, and, even if it does not have direct support from the chronicles, it certainly does not conflict with any of them. The baggage train was tied to the wood to the north of town, probably on the reverse-slope of the hill. Several sources describe the baggage trains as being formed into some sort of defensive perimeter with the horse at its centre, and included in the trains there were to be found, apparently, at least a few primitive cannon, which served as little more than noise-makers.

The English army was thus arrayed when Philip sent his scout party forward to investigate. Jean le Bel tells us that in the last hours before the battle, King Edward visited his men in their positions, encouraging them, and commanding them to hold fast in their positions. They had dug small pits to their front, which served to break up the inevitable French cavalry charges.[60] Froissart indicates that all was set by late morning, and that Edward and his men enjoyed a good meal and even a drink (presumably of wine) before the French arrived.[61] The mood was very different from what the English would experience in the hours before the battle at Poitiers.

Philip's army had marched out of Abbeville that morning, also in high spirits, after having celebrated mass.[62] The French king sent forward a reconnaissance force to locate Edward's position. When it reported back to him (after he had marched 3 leagues) that the English were only four more leagues (12 miles) to his front, he sent forth a smaller group of more distinguished knights to reconnoitre the disposition of Edward's force.[63] Froissart lists their names as the Lord Moyne of Bastleberg (from the king of Bohemia's party), and the lords of Noyers, Beaujeu and Aubigny.[64] Le Bel identifies only their leader with a curiously similar name: the Monk of Bazeilles.[65] As the French scouts came into view of the English arrayed for battle, they noted that Edward had formed three divisions (though they did not discuss their arrangement) and returned with their report to Philip, advising him to spend the rest of the afternoon reconsolidating his forces in order to more effectively attack the next morning. The French

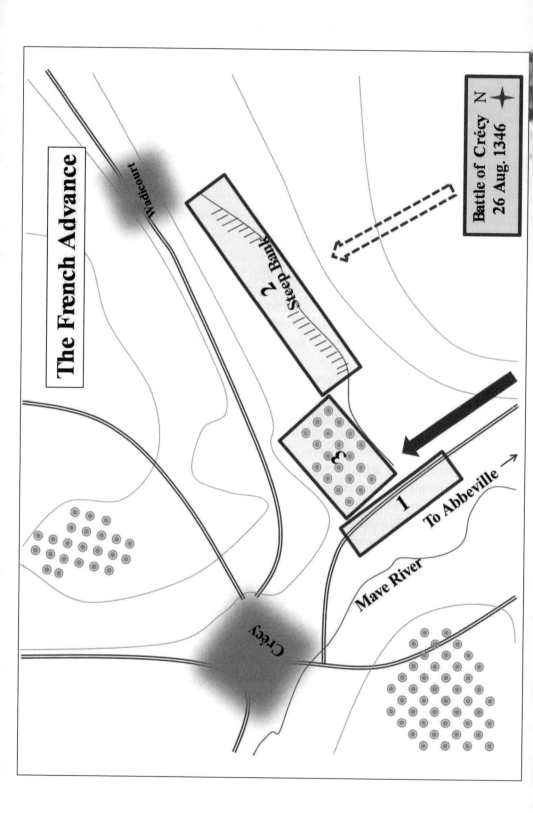

The French Advance

Battle of Crécy N
26 Aug. 1346

Wadicourt

Steep Bank

2

3

1

To Abbeville →

Mave River

Crécy

knights, however, finding themselves close to an enemy so long denied them, could not be restrained and the long-awaited assault was underway.[66]

In a scene that we shall see replicated in the opening moves of Poitiers, there was a rush among the French knights to be at the forefront of the action. Recognizing the tactical value of disrupting the English formation before unleashing the heavy cavalry charge into their ranks, Philip advanced his Genoese crossbowmen. At this point, in another example of divine providence interceding on Edward's behalf, a violent thunderstorm erupted but dissipated quickly. When the afternoon sun broke through, it shone into the eyes of the advancing forces of the French king.[67] The Genoese objected that the rain had rendered their weapons useless.[68] Those that could, fired at the English, whose longbowmen answered in kind, though with far more effect. Froissart describes the acumen of the English archers as being with such 'force and quickness that it seemed as if it snowed'.[69] Those crossbowmen who were able, fled, probably back to the small wood to their rear. Others were pinned between the advancing French cavalry and the English position and suffered the wrath of both.[70]

At this point the French knights, apparently under the nominal command of the Duke of Alençon, began a series of charges directly into what would, in today's military parlance, be described as the *engagement area* or, more suitably, the *kill zone*. The only way the French knights could hope to break the English formation would be to get within striking distance with their personal arms. At that proximity the mounted knight would enjoy significant advantages over the dismounted, poorly armoured and equipped – and poorly trained – archer or foot soldier. But to get that close, he would first have to survive the hail of armour-piercing arrows from thousands of archers, whose range would fast become point-blank. Le Bel's description of the scene is the most vivid:

The [battalions] of the great lords were so inflamed by envy, one against another, that they did not wait for one another, but attacked completely disordered and mixed together without any order whatsoever so that they trapped the light infantry and the Genoese between them and the English so that they could not flee. Thus the weak horses fell over them, and the others trampled them, and they tumbled over each other like pigs in a heap. On the other side the archers fired so marvellously that when the horses felt these barbed arrows (which did wonders), some would not go forwards, others leapt into the air as if maddened, others balked and bucked horribly, others turned their rumps towards the enemy, regardless of their masters, because of the arrows they felt. Some, unable to avoid it, let themselves fall. The English lords, who were on foot, advanced and pierced through these men, who could not help themselves, by their own efforts or by their horses.[71]

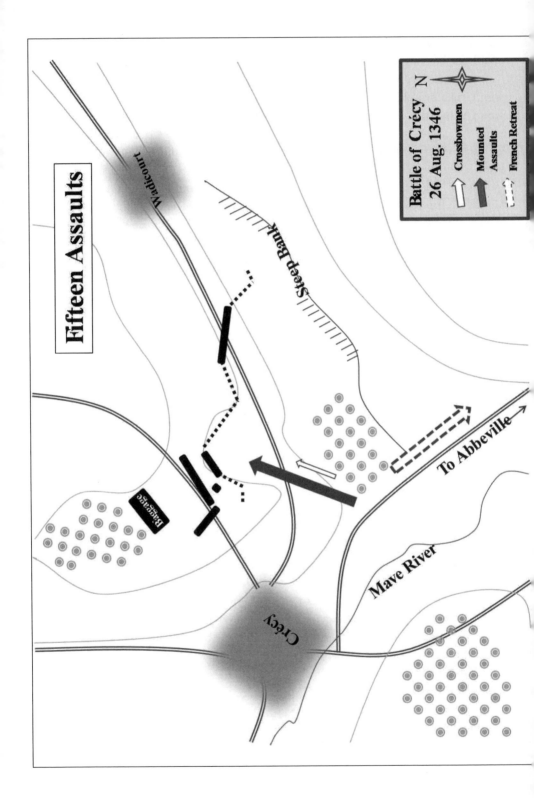

Fifteen Assaults

Battle of Crécy
26 Aug. 1346

N

Crossbowmen
Mounted Assaults
French Retreat

Wadicourt

Steep Bank

Baggage

Crécy

Mave River

To Abbeville

The Lessons of Crécy

The episode did not deter further French charges into the fray. It is possible that the sheer number of attackers contributed to the confusion so much that successive waves were not aware of the one-sidedness of the slaughter, but more likely they believed that they could overcome Edward's defence, or at least that their honour demanded that they try. Philip had assembled an immense army, filled with most of the greatest lords in that part of Europe. They each had come to participate in a heroic battle and enhance their personal glory. Perhaps the most famous example of adherence to this culture is found in the actions of the blind (or nearly so) King Charles of Bohemia, who demanded that he be led into the fight so that he could strike Englishmen with his sword. He was later found dead with his attendants, their horses still lashed together.[72] Philip surely felt that he could not retreat. His reputation had already suffered too much to this point, since he had avoided battle for so long, permitting his kingdom to be so thoroughly despoiled. The charges continued. Philip had at least one horse killed beneath him, and may have even received an arrow wound in his face.[73]

Though the fight was wearing down the English – and at one point Prince Edward was in grave personal danger – the French situation only worsened with time. Night's darkness had set, but lighted by a bright moon French knights conducted as many as fifteen charges. These would have been over ground increasingly littered with bodies of men and horses, some injured, some dead, and with steadily deteriorating coordination in the attack. As midnight approached, Philip, enraged and probably despairing in the moment of this unforeseen catastrophe, wanted to lead a sixteenth charge. The commander typically led the reserve. Ten years later, at Poitiers, the commander of each side would lead his reserve in a desperate attempt to salvage a victory. Philip never entered the fight, however. Jean of Hainault took his horse by the reins and led the French king to safety.[74] Edward's soldiers, exhausted, slept in their battle positions, not even removing their armour, in case the French regrouped and assaulted the hill anew. King Edward, who had watched the battle from a windmill north-west of the prince's location, paid his son tribute for his performance that day, saying: 'Sweet son, God give you good perseverance: you are my son, for most loyally you acquitted yourself this day: you are worthy to be a sovereign.'[75]

Philip did not renew his assault, but the following morning the dismounts who had stretched the length of the road back to Abbeville finally arrived. Le Baker reports that these fresh troops conducted the sixteenth charge, but were no more successful than the previous attempts had been. Now the English pursuit began and an additional 3,000 Frenchmen were killed.[76] Heralds scoured the fields, determining the identities of the fallen as best they could. They listed over 1,500 knights among the dead, including two kings, nine princes, an

41

archbishop and eight earls.[77] Very few English casualties are reported. Knighton notes the death of only three knights[78] and le Baker writes that 'only forty of the king's whole army were found to have been killed'.[79] Le Bel offers the more reasonable number of '300 English knights dead'.[80]

The number of English casualties, however, does little to add to or diminish the critical impact of the battle. Crécy was a disaster for Philip. He had approached the fight as the clear favourite but had lost perhaps 10,000–15,000 men and done inestimable damage to his reputation. Edward marched on to Calais, and sat before its walls for eleven months. During that time Philip had great difficulty in raising an army to lead against him again. When he did march to the relief of Calais, he faced a much larger English army than he had at Crécy, and it was in a much more defensible position. Not wishing to repeat his mistake, Philip abandoned his beleaguered citizens. The city fell, and would serve as the one constant English foothold in the north for 100 years to come. Edward had marched through Philip's kingdom, challenged him, and won. Less than two months later, events in England would only add to Philip's strategic woes.

Analysis and Conclusions

The preceding description of the events that led to and occurred during the fighting of the battle of Crécy may seem, perhaps, more in-depth than is merited in a study of the Poitiers campaign. Poitiers cannot, however, as either a campaign or a battle be correctly understood in the absence of key preceding events. Even contemporaries of the two battles understood the significance of the Black Prince's experiences at Crécy. Geoffrey le Baker accordingly links the two events inextricably:

> In this desperate battle, Edward of Woodstock, the king's eldest son, aged sixteen, displayed marvellous courage against the French in the front line, running through horses, felling knights, crushing helmets, cutting lances apart, avoiding enemy's missiles; as he did so, he encouraged his men, defended himself, helped fallen friends to their feet, and set everyone an example; nor did he rest from his labours until the enemy retreated leaving behind a heap of dead bodies. There he learnt that knightly skill which he later put to excellent use at the battle of Poitiers.[81]

Surely Crécy gave the young prince, in addition to 'knightly skill', the knightly virtue of bravery; he never could have undertaken such a campaign as that which led him to the Maupertuis Plain if he had not already learned his father's craft in the journey through Normandy and on the fields of Crécy. But the chronicler errs by failing to notice that the most important lessons the Black Prince learned from his father were not in the realm of individual combat, but at the *operational level of war.* It is at this level that campaigns are conducted and sites for battles are selected. With this in mind, let us examine what the Black Prince learned from the Crécy campaign of 1346.

In the introduction I suggested that the young prince learned lessons that could be grouped into three basic categories:

Reluctant armies could be brought to battle given the right incentive

This is perhaps the most obvious, and, at the same time, most significant lesson that the Black Prince would take away from his experiences campaigning alongside his father and the other distinguished commanders of his day. There existed three basic campaign strategies available to King Edward: siege, devastation and battle. He had not landed on the Cotentin and marched through Normandy in order to reclaim those lands that had been part of the realm of the English kings in the day of William the Conqueror. That would have been a legitimate strategic objective and a fitting campaign strategy, but that was not his purpose. Had it been, he would have done more to garrison the castles and cities along the way, and he never would have advanced so near to Paris. He conducted very few sieges (Cherbourg, La Hogue, Carenten, Barfleur and Caen) and these were of significant strategic value and not at all protracted. He refused to besiege the much larger Rouen because of its size, but he could not have hoped to control Normandy without first capturing its capital.

Similarly, Edward was not merely raiding enemy territory with the hope of embarrassing his rival and then escaping without facing him in battle. He had expended too much capital – monetary and political – to return home without a major victory. There had been too many military failures among recent English kings, dating back to his great-great-grandfather, John Lackland, who had lost the Continental possessions to begin with, and his grandfather, Henry III, who had burdened English kings with fealty to their French adversaries since the Treaty of Paris in 1259. England, thus, was not yet sufficiently politically or economically mobilized to endure another fruitless campaign in France, particularly when the Scots still posed such a threat to the north of the kingdom. Edward's letter requesting supplies en route to Calais demonstrates that he understood the importance of achieving something significant on this foray. It is doubtful that he would have been satisfied with the conquest of the port of Calais in the absence of a great battle with Philip, but at least that would have been a measurable accomplishment that offered some financial compensation for England, and would have provided for future operations in the north of France. However, if Edward had reached Calais without first facing Philip in battle, the French king would surely have marched to its relief. He had already been raising an army to oppose Edward, and as it happened, Edward remained camped before the stubborn walls of Calais for eleven months, during which time Philip would certainly have attacked him.

Victory at Poitiers

Knowing this, the English king's planned march to Calais can be viewed as a final attempt to bring the reluctant French to a truly decisive battle. As it turned out, this would be unnecessary, because he had, by then, had his battle at Crécy.

The 16-year-old Black Prince observed all of this as it unfolded. The campaign, from the landing at La Hogue to the triumphal entrance through the gates of Calais, lasted about thirteen months. The prince thus had 400 nights of discussion on strategy and tactics – even when he was not personally present during much of the siege – to argue the merits of his father's campaign plans. He then had eight years for more deliberation and reflection before he embarked for Bordeaux to conduct his own campaign. He now knew how to bring the French king to battle, and he believed he knew how to win the battle. But was a battle what he wanted? Both Crécy and Calais were successes, they had accomplished their tactical objectives, but at the campaign level there was only limited success. Edward III had not achieved sovereignty of Gascony, nor had he succeeded in taking the crown of France for himself. Future operations would be necessary.

These battles were not only more likely to occur if the enemy trusted too heavily in his own weight of numbers, but that victory was more dependent upon tactical than numerical superiority

The French at Crécy were willing (even eager) to attack Edward despite his well-prepared defensive position because they believed that the significant numerical advantage they enjoyed (and the fact that they were mounted French knights) would more than compensate for the disadvantages inherent in the attack. Earlier, at Blanchetaque, as Philip's army chased Edward at the tidal ford crossing the Somme, the French recognized the folly of conducting an attack at that moment and wisely moved upstream to Abbeville, the nearest point at which he and his army could safely cross and continue their pursuit. As noted above, Philip made a similar decision when marching to the relief of Calais. Nearing the beset city almost a full year after his defeat at Crécy, he found that Edward had prepared an unassailable position. The English king certainly had had sufficient time to prepare his defences – he had been before the walls of Calais for nearly eleven months by the time Philip arrived, and had even constructed a fortified city, which he called 'Villeneuve-le-Hardi', opposite the port town he was besieging. There were only two routes that Philip could take to approach Edward's army, and the English king had prepared strong defences along both. Additionally, Edward had with him the single largest army that England deployed in the whole of the Middle Ages. Philip entreated Edward to allow the two armies to fight on a field that did not so clearly favour one side over the other, but Edward declined. In the end, Philip marched away, and the townspeople, already starving and forlorn, lowered the French flags from the battlements and requested terms for surrender.

The Lessons of Crécy

In this instance, Edward's position was too strong to entice Philip to attack. One may argue that Philip was predisposed to avoiding battle after the humiliating defeat he had suffered the last time the two monarchs had met. However, the wound was not so fresh in the summer of 1347. His shock and despair had turned to anger and shame, and he had raised a new army to confront Edward. Philip had marched from Paris to Calais for that very reason, and made several attempts to draw Edward onto the open plains so that he could avenge himself for his disgrace at Crécy. The Black Prince, recognizing that Philip truly did desire battle but that he would not attack such an insurmountable defence, would have noted that if he were in the future to attempt to entice an adversary to battle, he would have to find a delicate balance between his actual and apparent strength. If his position appeared too well devised, he would never succeed in causing his enemy to make the fatal error of assuming the tactical offence. The Black Prince learned from his father the tremendous advantage inherent in the tactical defence, and the young commander would not forget that lesson when the burden of decision rested on his own shoulders.

Battle, as 'the final arbiter' could empower a kingdom of lesser economy and population to overcome a stronger rival

The siege of Calais had been a very expensive enterprise. Despite the fact that in the coming years and decades Edward III would increasingly mobilize his kingdom's economy for war, England was still a very small kingdom compared to France, and had very limited resources, even with the expansion of the textile industry during this period. The nobles who sat for eleven months in 'Villeneuve-le-Hardi' must have grumbled among themselves about the excessive duration of the siege. They must have questioned whether their time and resources could have better been spent elsewhere. What good was all their training and tactical expertise? The city eventually surrendered peacefully – Philip's relief army would not even attack! Crécy had been a more noble pursuit. They ravaged the countryside for six weeks, growing rich off the lands that the French king would not protect, and then in one glorious evening, they destroyed a numerically superior army full of the most famous knights of Western Europe. But what had it gotten them? Had it truly brought Edward closer to the French crown, or even to an independent Gascony? These questions would be asked again ten years later after the battle of Poitiers. Edward felt that the outcome of Crécy *had* brought him closer to achieving his strategic goals. One more battle of that sort and Philip and the elite of France would grant him his every request. It was just a matter of Edward being able to force the combat to take place at a time and on ground of his own choosing. He had very nearly broken France's back at Crécy. One more great contest and France would be his.

Neville's Cross

E ven as Crécy encouraged the young prince's pursuit of decisive combat, another battle, fought only six weeks later on the other extreme of Edward's kingdom reinforced the Black Prince's strategic thought. In the summer of 1346, Philip VI, annoyed at Edward III's devastation of the Cotentin and yet not desiring to immediately confront him in battle, instigated a Scottish invasion of England from the north. The French king hoped that a reply in kind for the English incursion into his own kingdom would force Edward to withdraw from the Continent. Philip was probably more willing that the Scots and English should face one another in a costly battle than that his own troops should participate, but he was also aware that the Scots were very capable of avoiding battle when necessary, as they had demonstrated years before against a younger Edward III.

In truth, though Philip probably would have been content with the removal of the English threat from Normandy, his plan did not stop there. It was not his design that the French should be on the defensive throughout the war. He, too, had strategic ambitions, including a permanent domination of the former Angevin empire and Gascon holdings, and a weakening of his greatest rival, England, which he would accomplish by strengthening her northern neighbour, Scotland. To this end, Philip promised David II of Scotland that he would land French troops in Cornwall to join efforts with the Scottish troops. The two armies could then create a pincer effect upon Edward's forces and annihilate them. The degree to which Philip was dedicated to this plan we will never know, but we can be certain that it would not have been executed according to his original designs. Among the captured at Caen in the beginning of August, 1346, was the Count of Eu, who was Constable of France, Philip's commander-designee for the amphibious invasion.

David, confident of his own command and of his ally's commitment to the strategy, swore that they would celebrate Christmas together in London. Philip's was by no means an unreasonable request; the raid would be the fourth such into English territory in two years. The French king's assurances of aid only made David even more enamoured of the prospect of invading England. Philip, according to the *Pakington Account*, promised that 'the realm of England was left denuded of men-at-arms, and so that no people worthy of concern were left in the said realm, except men of the Holy Church and shepherds'.[82] Fortunately for England, one of those men of the Holy Church was the Archbishop of York. Froissart, writing years later, did not share the same perception that England was void of military forces, though it must be admitted that he clearly benefited from hindsight. When describing King Edward's preparations before disembarking for the 1346 campaign, he reported that: 'he established the Lord Percy and the Lord Neville to be wardens of his realm with [the Archbishop of Canterbury,] the Archbishop of York, the bishop of Lincoln and the bishop of Durham; for he never voided his realm but that he left ever enough at home to keep and defend the realm, if need were.'[83] Froissart erred in listing the bishop of Durham among those left to 'defend the realm', for he, as we have seen, was certainly with Edward at Crécy, but this fact does not detract from the chronicler's point that not every able administrator and commander had accompanied the king abroad.

The Anglo-Scottish wars mirrored the English conflict with France to a remarkable degree, each case a smaller kingdom in a struggle for suzerainty, further complicated by succession crises and interference from foreign powers. Since the parties involved in each instance tailored their strategic pursuits to the requirements of each convoluted political situation, and the situations were similar in so many ways, it should be no surprise that the ensuing campaigns bore striking resemblances to one another. To consider this issue a step further, modern historians must not underestimate the powers of perception of the contemporary witnesses to both of these wars. Edward III, and naturally his son, the Black Prince, as well as many of their advisors, surely recognized the similarities, weighed the usefulness of such comparisons, and applied the lessons learned as they deemed beneficial.

The three kingdoms, England, Scotland and France, were inextricably tied. Alexander III of Scotland had married Margaret of England, sister of Edward I ('Longshanks'). The queen mother was Eleanor of Provence, sister of the then king of France, St Louis IX. Edward I's second wife was the young Marguerite, daughter of Philip III of France, only 16 years old at her wedding to the 60-year-old monarch. Edward II, who assumed the throne of England upon his father's death in 1307, married Isabella of France, daughter of Philip IV, his own stepmother's niece. Edward III married Philippa of Hainault, granddaughter of Philip III of France, his mother's first cousin. When Alexander III of Scotland died in a riding accident in 1286, he left the throne vacant without a clear heir. Though he was only 44 at the time of his death, he had outlived all three of his children. He had recently remarried to Yolande de Dreux, who was pregnant when Alexander died, but the pregnancy did not reach full term. The closest heir was Alexander's granddaughter, Margaret, but she, too, died before she could take the crown. Scotland fell into a four-year interregnum period until two clear claimants to the throne emerged: John Balliol of Galloway and Robert the Bruce of Annandale. Balliol was the great-great-great-grandson of David I of Scotland; Robert the Bruce was one generation further removed. After two additional years of contest, the Scots submitted to Edward I's judgment on the matter in an attempt to establish an enduring resolution. Edward decided in favour of Balliol, but forced the Scots to acknowledge the English king as overlord. Thus, by the end of the thirteenth century, Edward I had as a vassal a foreign king, just as he himself, as Duke of Aquitaine, was vassal to the king of France. Robert died in 1329, when his son, David II, was only 5 years old. David ruled, with the interposition of Edward Balliol from 1332–1336, until he died without heir in 1371, six years before the death of Edward III.

When considering the similarities between David's *chevauchée* into northern England in 1346 and the Black Prince's *chevauchées* through southern France in 1355–1356, one must first examine the motives of each commander. In his essay 'Disaster at Neville's Cross: the Scottish Point of View', historian Alexander S. Grant identified four factors that contributed to the Scottish undertaking. The first of these is essentially retributive. The English held Scottish territories that Robert sought to liberate. A foreign king had seized part of his birthright, and he wanted to take it back. Now consider the Black Prince's position in 1355. Gascony, a fief passed down through his family for over 200 years was now being wrested from his hands by the Count of Armagnac in the name of the king of France. Gascony was the prince's land as much as was the much nearer and newly-won princedom of Wales. It was, in fact, the largest and most profitable portion of his inheritance, and he would not countenance its loss.

Grant's second factor is at first glance less directly applicable to the Black Prince's 1355–1356 campaigns, but merits consideration. He argues that David was forced to conduct a bold military manoeuvre to quell domestic challenges to his authority. David was young, only 22 during the campaign, and his prestige had yet to be established. The most effective way at the time for a young royal to enhance his standing was via a demonstration of military strength. As a result, the young Scottish king assembled as many of his vassals as he could, and marched in defiance of the usurper of his lands. The Black Prince faced a similar situation in 1355. Armagnac had taken advantage of the outbreak of the Hundred Years War to assert his own dominance over much of the English holdings in Gascony. The 25-year-old prince answered with a campaign of legendary success. In 1346 David Bruce feared losing his kingdom to the many rival factions within, but it was just a fear – one that proved unfounded since he did not lose his throne even during his many years of captivity after the disaster at Neville's Cross. Nine years later, however, the Black Prince was watching his inheritance get gobbled up by Philip's lieutenant in the south, the Count of

Armagnac. A lord who could not protect his vassals would soon find himself to be no lord at all. Prince Edward had to act quickly before local leaders deserted their traditional anglophile tendencies.

Grant's third reason for David's invasion cites the matter of international strategic concerns. The Scottish king had obligated himself to Philip to invade England if it threatened France. Not only was David thus honour-bound to fulfil the terms of this treaty, but, as Grant points out, since Philip had just lost so decisively at Crécy, if he did not act quickly, Philip might come to terms with Edward independent of David, leaving the Scots as the sole focus of English military action. This dilemma, too, has its parallel for the Black Prince in 1355. The south of France was a region over which no monarch had yet been able to solidify his rule. The local leaders were powerful and of independent spirit. Much of the reason that they favoured English governance over French was that the farther away their king lived, the greater their local liberties. However, the basic role of any government is to protect the governed, and Edward would have to maintain sufficient strength in Gascony to rebuff incursions from French and Spanish designs, alike. These obligations pulled him into the struggle for control of Aquitaine as much as David's agreements with Philip compelled him to act in the early autumn of 1346.

The fourth and final reason Grant gives for David's invasion of 1346 was that it 'was simply too good to miss'. This factor, too, must have been present in the Black Prince's mind as he, nine years later, rode unchallenged from Bordeaux nearly to the Mediterranean coast. Jean, now king of France, had demonstrated that he no more sought a battle than had his father a decade before. The country south of the River Garonne was as bare of resistance as had been the region north of the Humber for Robert, and even more so, as evidenced by the lack of any major confrontation. Edward III had correctly assessed the strategic situation in Gascony when he ordered the 1355 *chevauchée*, and he and the Black Prince cannot have missed the similarities between the raid that had culminated at Neville's Cross and their own plans for a far more successful campaign.

As much as the Neville's Cross campaign would inspire the Black Prince, the Crécy campaign must first have been an inspiration to David Bruce. Edward III, only months earlier, had invaded lands that had once been held by his ancestors, and had succeeded not only in embarrassing the French king by devastating so much of the lands under his alleged protection, but was currently laying siege to the important port town of Calais, in an attempt to gain a permanent foothold on the Continent.

On 1 October, just five weeks after the French catastrophe at Crécy, David assembled his forces at Perth. Two days later they crossed the English border and began their devastation of the border counties. While it is unlikely that

Neville's Cross

David was well-informed regarding the events at Crécy when he began his own campaign, he surely knew that Edward III was absent with the greater part of his best knights, and must have relished the opportunity to mirror Edward's campaign against Philip by ravaging England at the very same time. John Leland's contribution to the *Scalachronica* indicates that the Scottish *chevauchée* entered England along two axes of advance, through Carlisleshire and Solway. David's first target of note was the fortress of Liddel, whose defence had been entrusted to Lord Walter of Selby. After a three-day siege, the Scots stormed the fortifications and massacred its garrison. They 'assaylid the pile of Lidel and wan it by assaute, and then cut of the hedde of Walter Selby capitayne there' in plain view of the rest of the defenders, reinforcing their notoriously harsh treatment of those who dared resist. From here David once again split his army along two separate lines of march. Having determined that the primary mission of the *chevauchée* was to devastate the north counties in order to gain bargaining power for Scottish independence while Edward and his army were abroad, David sought to create the widest possible swath of destruction he could before the campaign season ended.

The Scottish king was attacking at a very favourable moment. Not only could he expect resistance to be light, but he knew that larders and barns would be full, as the harvest was just coming in. David led the greater part of his force east against Lanercost and Hexham. A smaller contingent turned back towards Redpath, ravaged Redesdale, and then rejoined the main body at Hexham. After spending three days at Hexham Abbey, David continued the march south. At the head of 2,000 choice men-at-arms and as many as 17,000 light troops, the Bruce marched through Ryton and Ebchester en route to his target destination of York and, ostensibly, London. On 14 October, David's army arrived at Bear Park, also called Beaupaire Manor, outside Durham. Edward III, himself, had stopped at Durham nearly twenty years earlier during his 1327 Weardale campaign. The large town was a logical stop along any Scottish invasion route, just under 60 miles from York, the next probable objective in David's raid. The Scot had no reason to expect anything but continued success. Far from encountering stiff resistance, his march met only with throngs of local landowners, bearing gifts and tribute for the Scottish king in exchange for amnesty from his campaign of devastation. According to the Lanercost chronicler, David benefited doubly from these payments. The Scottish king may have permitted the towns of Hexham, Corbridge, Darlington and Durham to stand even without paying ransom, because he 'intended to obtain his victual from them in the winter season'. It was yet another 250 miles to London, but he had covered a distance nearly half that far already, and he had only been on the march for two weeks. He still had over two months to make good his vow to occupy London by Christmas, and Philip's reports about the defencelessness of the English realm seemed to be accurate.

Victory at Poitiers

As David's fast-moving army rolled ever south, it was no surprise that the inhabitants of the English north country should seek to buy the Scots' goodwill rather than oppose them militarily, just as the Normans had offered money to Edward III. The invaders were respected as warriors to be feared. Chronicler Jean Froissart, who was born the same year that the war broke out, records popular opinion of the Scots as no modern historian could adequately summarize:

> These Scottish men are right hardy and sore travailing in harness and in wars. For when they will enter into England, within a day and a night they will drive their whole host twenty-four miles, for they are all a horseback, unless it be the followers and laggards of the host, who follow afoot. The knights and squires are well horsed, and the common people and others on little hackneys and geldings; and they carry with them no carts or chariots because of the diversities of the mountains that they must pass through in the country of Northumberland. They take with them no provision of bread or wine, for their usage and soberness is such in time of war that they pass in the journey a great long time with flesh half cooked, without bread, and drink of the river water without wine, and they neither care for pots nor pans, for they see the beasts in their own skins [...] Wherefore it is no great marvel though they make greater journeys than other people do. And in this manner were the Scots entered into the county and wasted and burnt all about as they went, and took great number of beasts.

Thus the invading Scots would have been an imposing threat under any circumstances, but with the English king and his army abroad and no one left to protect them, the townspeople did what they could to survive.

Meanwhile, the English forces under Archbishop William de la Zouche were gathering at York. Though, as David knew, most of the most prominent noblemen were on campaign with Edward in France, many had stayed behind, perhaps anticipating another Scottish invasion. These few now rallied their men in defence of the realm, their ranks boasting some celebrated soldiers. The commanders subordinate to de la Zouche included: Henry Percy, Raymond Neville, Gilbert d'Umphraville, John Mowbray, Ralph Hastings, Thomas Rokesby (sheriff of Yorkshire), John Kirkby (bishop of Carlisle), Thomas Lucy, the chronicler Thomas Gray, William Deyncourt, Robert Ogle, Robert Bertram, John Coupland, and the Lords Maulay, Scrope, Musgrave, Leybourne and Ferrers. Local communities, encouraged by de la Zouche's efforts, rallied against the Scots. To the English host Yorkshire contributed fifteen men-at-arms, twenty-nine hobelars and 3,020 horse-archers. Lancashire supplied four knights, sixty men-at-arms, 960 horse-archers and 240 dismounted archers. The counties of Durham, Cumberland, Westmoreland and Northumberland also sent men, numbering perhaps another 4,000–5,000. Since the knights, men-at-arms and hobelars would have attendant retinues not included in the count, the total numbers were actually much higher than recorded: 10,000–12,000 is a reasonable estimate for the English assembled at York by 4 October. From there they passed through Richmond on their great northward march.

The same day that David's reassembled army arrived to camp at Bear Park, de la Zouche's men reached Barnard Castle, only 20 miles away. On the 16th, the English conducted a night march to Bishop Auckland, to a park just over half the distance to the Scottish position, where they set up camp and prepared for the coming battle. The Scots were, at this point, unaware of the exact disposition of any resistance, but an army so large could not hope to escape their detection for long.

At first light one of the chief Scottish commanders, Sir William Douglas, leading a mounted reconnaissance of 500 troops, stumbled upon de la Zouche's men. The Lancrcost chronicler reports in dramatic fashion that it was the hand of God that delivered the Scots into English outstretched arms. He describes a thick fog engulfing Douglas and his men just before they were set upon by a great number of English knights. Douglas lost 300 men in the brief encounter with the English divisions under the Archbishop and Sir Thomas Rokesby, and hurried back to warn David that his advance would not be nearly so unchallenged as previously anticipated. He was chased by Robert Ogle almost the entire way back to the camp. The exchange that occurred between the captain and his king has been passed down to us, and even if it is not an exact transcript of the conversation that took place, it likely replicates the tenor of the exchange:

> 'David! Arise quickly; see! All the English have attacked us!' But David declared that it could not be so. 'There are no men in England,' said he, 'but wretched monks, lewd priests, swineherds, cobblers, and skinners. They dare not face me: I am safe enough.' 'Assuredly,' replied William, 'oh dread king, by your leave if you will, it is otherwise. There are diverse valiant men (among them); they are advancing quickly upon us and mean to fight.'

Thus alerted to the fact that a great English host was only a short march from his position, David readied his defence. He had not expected to do battle when he began this invasion, but still believing that all the best English commanders were abroad in France, he did not now shrink from the opportunity to fight an army foolish enough to attack him on ground of his own choosing. A victory over the English home guard promised not only to strengthen his position at the bargaining table, but also to enrich his men with ransoms won. Thus, early on the morning of the 17th, David moved forward from his camp at Bear Park to more defensible terrain.

The fields he found were well suited for his purposes, as long as he remained on the tactical defence. Either side of the selected battlefield bordered on swampy marshland, providing flank security against even infantry, and was probably untrafficable for any mounted forces. The centre field itself was little better for manoeuvre purposes, and, while David has been heavily faulted for his choice of terrain, it must be remembered that he was selecting a site from which to defend, not one on which he planned to launch an attack. The Scots, like the French and English, had seen enough of warfare to recognize the tremendous inherent strength of the tactical defence. A clever commander would thus endeavour to select suitable terrain and then force his enemy to attack him. Though David had to some extent been forced to accept the fields north of Neville's Cross, so long as he remained on the defence, his choice was sound. To his great misfortune, this was not to be.

The Scots hurriedly drew up into battle formation in three divisions. David assigned Patrick, Earl of Dunbar, to command the first division. His refusal of this post and subsequent assumption of the rear command should have portended to David of things to come. John Randolph, Earl of Moray, and William Douglas thus assumed the honour of commanding the first division. Many of Scotland's finest knights joined those front ranks, including the Earls of Stratherne and Fife, John Douglas and William Ramsay. The king led the second division and was accompanied by the Earls of Buchan and Menteith, as well as Malcolm Fleming and Sir Alexander Straghern. Robert Stewart and Dunbar led the third. The English also formed into three divisions, again with the commander in the centre. Sir Henry Percy, accompanied by Gilbert d'Umphraville, the Earl of Angus, Sir Ralph Neville and Sir Henry Scrope led in the first. De la Zouche commanded the second. Sir John Mowbray, Sir Thomas Rokesby and John Coupland fought in the third.

The face-off began early in the morning and lasted the entire day. By 9 a.m. each army had arrayed itself on terrain it determined to defend. Understandably, neither wished to give up that advantage by mounting an attack. There they sat for over five hours. Recognizing the advantage of the longbow's range, the English commanders ordered a contingent of 500 archers forward (1) to harass the Scottish lines. The Scots attempted to reply in kind (2), but their bows had not the range of the English longbows, and their archers had to retreat (3). It is likely that the hail of well-directed yard-long arrows did more than merely harass the Scottish soldiers. In the mid-fourteenth century, most armour would not have offered complete protection from the projectiles fired in such numbers. The French and allied army fighting at the same time at Crécy had learned this lesson at a steep price, and the wealthy Continental royalty assembled there

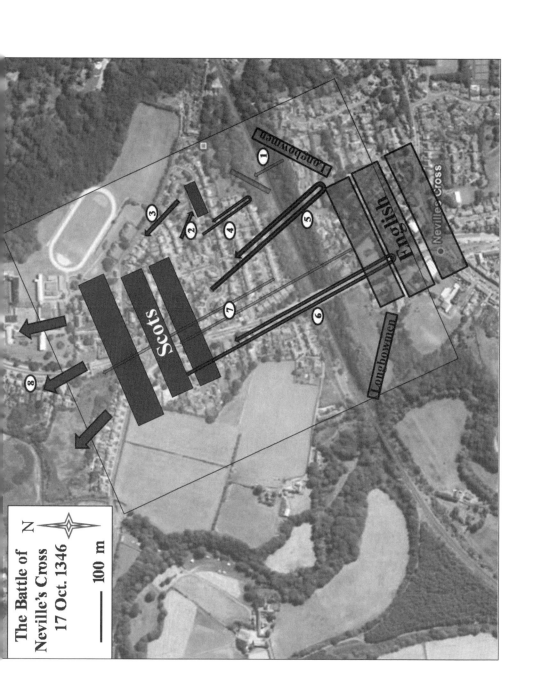

The Battle of Neville's Cross
17 Oct. 1346

N

100 m

Longbowmen
Longbowmen

English

Scots

Neville's Cross

surely could afford better armour than perhaps anyone on the field at Neville's Cross. But, like the army assembled at Crécy, there stood some men who did not respect the weapon's capabilities.

The Scottish Earl of Menteith, John Graham, understood that they had no recourse against the longbowmen other than to close the distance between them with a violent charge and drive them from the field. Thus, he lobbied for the honour of leading such a charge at the head of 100 mounted men-at-arms. His request refused, he rode forward alone. He made it further than many probably expected (4), but was forced to return to the main Scottish lines, his horse eventually shot from under him. Emboldened by Graham's actions, Moray's dismounted division moved forward against the right flank of the English first division, under Percy (5). These men, with the support of wings of longbowmen on the flanks, defeated this first charge. The Scottish first division recoiled, and, returning to the main formation, fell in with the men of David's division, which likewise rushed forward against de la Zouche's army (6). This second assault, made by the second Scottish division and augmented by the survivors of Moray's division, pushed the English formation back but could not break through.

As the Scots again recoiled, English archers advanced to fire at the retreating divisions and loosed their arrows on the untested Scottish reserve. The *Historia Roffensis Account* reports that 'the English archers surrounded the Scots so that they were not able to raise their heads'. The English divisions now rushed forward in a counter-attack (7), followed by a second, which had even greater success. Robert Stuart and the Earl of March, who, it must be remembered, had refused the honour of commanding David's lead division, now fled the field (8), taking the reserve with them and abandoning their king and the remnant of his army. David, by all accounts, fought valiantly. Sir John Coupland engaged him in hand-to-hand combat and captured him only after the Scot had been twice wounded in the face by arrows. The battle, now entering the early evening hours, was finally over. The fighting had been so fierce and so protracted that the two sides had actually agreed to three separate pauses 'for rest so as to fight again more strongly'.

David's fellow captives included Sir William Douglas and the Earls of Fife, Menteith and Wigtown. Robert Earl of Moray and Maurice Earl of Stratherne, as well as the constable, the chancellor and the chamberlain of Scotland were among the thousands who had died. Most of the captured knights were ransomed but David was kept safe in the Tower of London. He remained King Edward III's prisoner for eleven years – until after the battle of Poitiers. John Graham, who had valiantly led the first charge of the battle, was convicted as a traitor, hanged, drawn and quartered, and his limbs, according to the Lanercost chronicler, 'sent to various places in England and Scotland'.

Neville's Cross

And what was the impact of the Neville's Cross campaign? Some have argued that it was not a decisive battle because it did not forever settle the Anglo-Scottish dispute. However, David's capture did end any serious threat to Edward's northern border for a considerable length of time, and, coupled with the English victories at Crécy and Calais, inestimably enhanced Edward's prestige, as well as his strategic position with regard to his bid for the crown of France. There was also an economic effect. Historian Michael Prestwich notes that Edward III's war expenditures recorded in the king's *Wardrobe Accounts* amounted to £242,162 between 1344 and 1347. David II's ransom of 100,000 marks (£66,667), then, would have covered only one-fourth of the cost, but de la Zouche's expenses would have been only a fraction of the king's in Normandy, the bulk of which were accrued during the siege of Calais. The Archbishop's army was much smaller and in the field for a far shorter period. Additionally, Edward's Continental *chevauchée* had amassed a tremendous amount of plunder, and the acquisition of Calais, not to mention the damage caused to Philip's prestige, cannot be measured in monetary terms. But perhaps these were not the most significant ramifications of the battle of Neville's Cross. When the Black Prince returned from his father's victorious year-long foray into France, he met with David, he spoke with him and with English participants in the campaign. They exchanged stories and undoubtedly commented on their own performances (and, of course, those of their adversaries) time and again. This discourse did much to mould the young prince's military education. He learned, among other lessons, that a campaign of devastation could bring a reluctant army to battle, that numbers were not so important as their tactical employment on appropriate terrain, and that fighting from the tactical defence could help overcome other significant disadvantages.

Analysis and Conclusions

Reluctant armies could be brought to battle given the right incentive
The Black Prince learned this lesson by observing both the Scots and the English. Scottish commanders had made a practice of avoiding direct combat with English armies superior in number and equipment. Instances of this strategy abound throughout the reigns of the three Edwards. All it took to bring the Scots to battle was to inspire in them the belief that they could win. Edward III had very publicly sailed to France with the vast majority of his most capable knights. David knew this and sought to take advantage of the situation by running roughshod through northern England, hoping he might make it all the way to London. David, like most of his predecessors, did not share the Plantagenet desire to confront his mortal enemies in combat. He preferred, very rationally, to fight only when resistance would be minimal. Even when he

encountered de la Zouche's army outside Durham, he probably would not have fought if not forced into battle. Neither the tactical situation nor his sense of honour would permit him to retreat from this challenge, no matter how unexpected or how unwelcome.

Viewing the English from the opposite perspective of the campaign, one might consider that they, too, had the battle thrust upon them. While some among the English camp may have been desirous of battle, or at least eager to put an end to the constant ravages of the Scots, they surely realized their most dependable commanders and warriors were across the Channel seeking battle with the armies of France. They would likely have welcomed the addition of the deployed troops to their number as they rode north to face David's invaders. However, the Scottish incursion was not to be ignored. The further they allowed the raid to progress, the more the home guard would be discredited and the more English lands would be seized or consumed.

The Scots fought at Neville's Cross because they expected an easy victory from the outset of the campaign and because David fell victim to de la Zouche's surprising audacity. The men of England fought because their lands had been ravaged too often in the recent past and the security of the realm had been entrusted to their hands. The young Prince Edward would have heard campaign stories from both his English comrades and the Scottish captives after the battle and his return from France. The strategic implications of what he learned, together with his personal experience from the Crécy campaign, would have left indelible marks on his own strategic outlook.

These battles were not only more likely to occur if the enemy trusted too heavily in his own weight of numbers, but victory was more dependent on tactical than numerical superiority

Historians have long credited the Scots as fearsome warriors, but have not been generous enough with their praise of Scottish generals during their long struggle for independence from England. The Scottish commanders of the early fourteenth century understood that one should never willingly fight a battle on the enemy's terms. David had not undertaken the autumn campaign of 1346 in order to bring Edward to battle. His motives were different from those of the English king's own foray into Normandy. They were quite the opposite, in fact. David sought to take advantage of the *absence* of any notable defensive force. His plan was to devastate as much of northern England as possible en route to London, perhaps to join an army under the Count of Eu along the way. The first two weeks had progressed according to his plan, but then he found himself confronted by the formidable sight of several thousand Englishmen. Even then, however, he did not believe that victory had escaped him. In recent decades the Scots had proven themselves more than an even match for their southern neighbours, in victories such as those at Loudon Hill and Bannockburn. The fact that more recently the English had prevailed at Dupplin Moor and Halidon Hill may have made David more reluctant to engage in battle, but they could just as well have spurred him to defend his martial honour, especially if the army he now faced was, as he believed, denuded of experienced fighting men.

Battle, as 'the final arbiter', could empower a kingdom of lesser economy and population to overcome a stronger rival

David had not anticipated a decisive battle when he began his march from Perth at the beginning of October. His expectations for the campaign probably included a great, destructive raid, from which he would profit in terms of booty, ransom and honour. The Scottish king clearly planned on conducting a few minor sieges along his way to London, where he hoped to join the army of his French allies for Christmas. His forces were well-composed to conduct a massive battle, but with Edward and his choicest knights away in France, David anticipated no serious challenge to his *chevauchée*. If the English did mount any attempt at armed defence, the Scots were not merely prepared, but eager, to accept the challenge. David understood that battle possessed unequalled potential for sudden finality. Sieges, which could last years, necessitated of the besiegers lengths of service that were difficult for a feudal army to secure. Additionally, few medieval kingdoms were devised to provide the long-term logistical and pecuniary support required for such operations. Another alternative to battle, negotiations, resulted, by their very nature, in compromise. A king with a powerful army could hope to impose his will upon his neighbour in an exceptionally brief period – perhaps only a matter of hours (not including all of the training, preparations and manoeuvring, which should not be discounted). Battles often did not end in the 'winner take all' conclusions that each commander might have sought, but they possessed the potential to, and good commanders enter into battle aiming for the greatest possible outcome. David embarked upon his raid into the north of England in the autumn of 1346 without the expectation of battle. However, he was prepared for that eventuality and when the opportunity presented itself, he surely viewed it as good fortune because of the material advantages he enjoyed. In the end, the battle was decisive, but in ways contrary to all David's hopes and expectations. He was defeated by what was essentially England's home guard, and he spent the next decade in captivity.

1348–1355, War Between Battles

The kingdoms of England and France had few direct confrontations between 1346 and 1355. Those that did occur were typically between pro-English and pro-French vassals, and cannot be considered state-sponsored warfare. One of the most remarkable of these contests was the *Combat des Trente*, (Combat of the Thirty) fought in Brittany on 26 March 1351. At this battle, immortalized in verse, rather than two armies facing each other in their entireties, thirty English champions faced thirty French. They fought in view of both armies all day until the English, finally overcome with wounds and exhaustion, could fight no more. Many of their original number had died. But what could such a match have hoped to accomplish? Historian Jonathan Sumption asserts that *hastiludes* such as the Combat of the Thirty were 'symptoms of a war fought without strategic discipline or central control, by captains who were answerable only to themselves',[84] but as we shall see, there were also present throughout the Hundred Years War commanders who proved themselves very capable of strategic thought and unity of effort in complicated operations. In the mid-fourteenth century most of these men happened to be English, but French strategy during the second half of that century, dominated by Bertrand du Guesclin, proved both complex and effective.

Though it may have served no great strategic purpose, the Combat of the Thirty undoubtedly inspired Edward III and the Black Prince as much as it did the lesser nobles of the day. Similar combats between champions became more frequent in the years that followed, as those involved sought to achieve the same renown gained by participants of the original highly celebrated combat. Both Edwards (king and prince) were well-known adherents to the chivalric school. In the aftermath of the Crécy campaign, King Edward had founded the Royal Order of St George of the Garter. Among the twenty-four founding members, we find names familiar to those acquainted with Crécy and Poitiers: the Black Prince, the Earl of Suffolk, the Earl of Warwick, Henry of Grosmont, the Earl of Derby, and others besides. A kingdom's military power could be bolstered by the reputation of its knights. If the English were looking to augment their might with feats of arms and the foundation of chivalric orders, the French were of like mind. Jean II, in 1351, would mirror the Order of the Garter with his own institution of the Order of the Star.

By 1350 many Frenchmen must have been feeling disinherited by Providence. The Crécy campaign had stripped them not only of prestige and great expanses of land, but also of noblemen, who lay fallen in the English slaughter. Two years later the Black Death attacked members of every class, but the lowest suffered most heavily. Much is made of the 'opportunities' that this sudden drop in the labour force provided for the peasants who did survive, but the land-owning class was quick to provide for its own welfare, passing stringent laws that tied workers to the land and limited their wages to pre-plague levels. Of course, with an emasculated government and limited powers of law enforcement, the largely depopulated French countryside fell victim to acts of terror by roving bands. The situation was exacerbated by companies of English opportunists who sought to justify their pillaging as legitimate acts between warring kingdoms.

When King Philip VI died on 22 August 1350 and was succeeded by his son, Jean II (formerly the Duke of Normandy), some of his more powerful vassals decided to hedge their bets by negotiating directly with the king's greatest rival, Edward III. One such French vassal, Charles of Navarre, took advantage of Jean's precarious hold on the throne to extract from the new king a large fief on the Cotentin Peninsula as part of the Treaty of Mantes in 1354.[85] The next year, Charles turned to Edward to establish his own terms with the English sovereign. Jean learned of this treachery and arrested him on 5 April 1356, but this only drove the prisoner's supporters to espouse pro-English sympathies. Considering that Normandy was the part of France that lay closest to England, and that its possession had been hotly contested between the two kingdoms since the reign of Henry II, Jean had made a very inopportune choice in enemies.

Edward III, however, was no mean strategist. England faced obstacles of unthinkable proportion. Edward was in the midst of a complex two-front war against his northern neighbour, Scotland, and the far more powerful France. His kingdom had not yet entirely consolidated its holdings on the island, the frontier of Scotland never being better than uneasily quiet, and his possessions on the mainland of Europe were under constant threat of invasion. Like much of Europe, a great proportion of his subjects had suffered the ravages of the Black Death in 1348 and 1349. England's few Continental allies, the Flemish and the Navarrese in particular, were anything but constant in their support. In the face of these challenges, what did Edward decide to do? In 1355 he set in motion plans for a three-pronged invasion of France.

The English king's plan of attack largely resembled the campaign he had embarked upon nearly a decade before. One army would invade French possessions on the edges of his Duchy of Aquitaine, tying down forces in the south, while two other armies threatened Paris from the north and west. He depended upon foreign allies in no great measure in 1355. Though he would enlist the aid of loyal Gascons, these men, though not Englishmen, were the English king's subjects already. Edward likely hoped that at least two of his armies would be able to unite before engaging the French monarch in any large-scale battle, but he had defeated the French army once before without having achieved such a manoeuvre, and so would be confident he could repeat his success. Besides, two or three autonomous armies could be even more advantageous for the English cause than a united one. The consolidation of the invasion force into one host would allow the French to simplify their defence against a single massed army. Such a situation would only play to Jean's strengths, as the French already possessed a greater population of men from which to draw, and had all of the logistic advantages inherent in the defence. The more points at which the French were forced to defend, the easier it would be for the English to exploit any local numerical superiority they managed to achieve. The Black Prince would, of course, be eager to possess for the first time an independent command. Chandos' Herald recalls the scene in London as the prince, then 25 years old, entreated his father for the honour:

> One day said he to the king, his father, and to the queen, his mother: 'Sire, said he, by God's grace you know well that in Gascony the noble valiant knights love you so much that they take great trouble in your wars, and thereby enhance your honour; but they have no chieftain of your blood, as you know: wherefore if you like it, and by the aid of your counsel determine to send there one of your sons, they will be the more strong.' And everyone said that he spoke for the best. Then the king called, know for a truth, a meeting of his great Parliament. They were all unanimous to send the prince into Gascony, because of the high esteem in which he was held.[86]

In September of 1355, the Black Prince departed England for the Gascon capital of Bordeaux. There he and his father enjoyed strong support of the local aristocracy and merchant class. It was late in the campaign season and he would require time to raise Gascon forces before he could set his father's plan into motion. When Charles of Navarre withdrew his support for the English king at virtually the same moment as the prince landed in the south of France, the northern arms of the invasion, under Lancaster and King Edward, himself, had to reassess their plans of attack. Though the prince would conduct his raids through Languedoc without the direct support of friendly armies in the north, the threat of their invasion would paralyze Jean's forces in Normandy, resulting in a reduced threat to the English southern campaign. The Black Prince thus found himself in a situation remarkably similar to that of his father nine years before when he had ravaged Normandy, daring the French king to attack. For the English king and son no illusions existed. Jean could not countenance a repeat of his father's disgrace. A wholesale invasion of French territory would surely provoke an immediate reaction. It must be swiftly destroyed or at least repulsed. Enough strife persisted in Paris; a foreign invasion could not be tolerated. The Edwards expected battle.

The Black Prince's *chevauchée* of 1355, however, went unopposed. It had not lacked as a threat to Jean's power in southern France. Chandos' Herald provides a brief description of the extent of the destruction caused by the Anglo-Gascon army:

> At Bordeaux [the Black Prince] sojourned a while, until he had got together all his forces, and given his cavalry rest. Soon afterwards he made ready more than six thousand fighting men. He rode towards Toulouse; nor did he pass by any town, that he did not entirely ransack; and took Carcassonne, Beziers and Narbonne, and all the county was overrun and laid waste, as also many towns and castles; for which in Gascony the enemy had no reason to rejoice. We remained at this time in the field, for more than four months and a half, and there caused great disorder.[87]

The account, however, is slightly misleading. The prince and his army did sack many towns but primarily the portions laying outside the city walls. The suburbs of Carcassonne fell but never the castle. The 5,000 men of the Anglo-Gascon army destroyed everything in their path. Their objective was to create such devastation as to force Jean's hand and make him attack on unfavourable terms. At this point the prince was not endeavouring to annex Languedoc, so he did not dedicate any great length of time to the reduction of any formidable defences. As Alfred Burne notes, 'it was not the policy of the Black Prince to spend time and blood capturing places that he had no intention of holding'.[88]

At the same time, King Edward had crossed into France and once again took up his taunt of the French army, so that Jean was reluctant to commit any forces to a single battle. Still facing trouble with the Scots to the north, Edward returned his attention to that front. He was, however, no more successful at bringing the Scots to a decisive battle than he or his son had been with the French. Only two months after the end of the Black Prince's autumn campaign, the French king faced yet another threat. Lancaster invaded France with an English army and, unlike either of the Edwards, apparently came intent upon investing important towns. He sought to expand English influence with a greater permanence, rather than ravage the countryside. The Christmas season ushered in a period of small sieges, as the Black Prince and his lieutenants also seized or reduced Jean's fortifications in the south. The prince, obviously encouraged by the success of his autumn campaign demonstrated his disdain for the French opposition by dividing his already small force into four separate commands. The Captal de Buch, the renowned Gascon, took his contingent north towards Angoulême and Périgueux. Three of his captains, the Earls of Suffolk, Salisbury and Oxford, headed east along the Dordogne. His trusted advisor, the Earl of Warwick, moved south-east along the River Lot, and the prince himself campaigned with his friends, the young Chandos and Audley. These eight men not only did much to weaken Jean's political and pecuniary support in the south of France, but they would each play prominent roles in the campaign and battle of Poitiers.

The French king, for his part, found himself in an alarmingly precarious situation. His kingdom seemed to be crumbling beneath him. The three estates were ever reluctant to grant him the monies he required to raise a suitable army. His most promising ally, David of Scotland, was still imprisoned by their common enemy, Edward III. Bands of brigands were eroding civic authority even as English armies whittled away at his possessions, his income and his prestige. If he did not act, he would lose his kingdom, and whether it was to a foreign or a domestic threat mattered little. He initiated the steps necessary to field a force great enough to end the English incursions and hoped he would still have a kingdom to defend by the time he was able to employ it.

The Great Campaign

T he operations of 1355 had been very successful. The Black Prince had traversed southern France without opposition. The rewards were twofold. First, the members of the Anglo-Gascon army had greatly enriched themselves in material wealth and reputation. Many of the tales and the treasures alike had made their way back to the jubilant island. In much the opposite way, the French had suffered losses in both revenue and reputation. The loss of all of the gold, jewellery and other goods seized during the *chevauchée* was not the full measure of financial hardship created. Perhaps even greater was the loss of future tax revenue. This component was certainly felt more sharply by the crown. Just as there had been times when Scottish raids into the north counties had prevented English kings from collecting taxes in the newly-impoverished regions, now Jean faced a greatly diminished income just as he was confronted with an increased threat to his very rule. Sir John Wingfield, one of the prince's subordinate commanders during the *chevauchée*, described the situation in detail in a letter to the bishop of Winchester, then Treasurer of England:

> It seems certain that since the war against the French king began, there has never been destruction in a region as in this raid. For the countryside and towns which have been destroyed in this raid produced more revenue for the king of France in aid of his wars than half his kingdom [...] For Carcassonne and Limoux, which is as large as Carcassonne, and two other towns near there, produce for the king of France each year the wages of a thousand men-at-arms and 100,000 old *écus* towards the costs of war.[89]

The Black Prince was surely proud of his accomplishments in the previous year, but he must also have felt a certain amount of frustration. He had wanted to prove himself as a commander, but had been denied any significant opportunity to do so in the manner he most desired. The *chevauchée* had not brought Jean to battle, nor had the capture of so many fortifications on the Gascon march. The prince, encouraged by his father still in England, would undertake something far more daring. He would ride north into the very heart of France, join with the armies of his father and Lancaster, defeat the French king in battle, and see his father rightfully crowned in Rheims Cathedral. They were ambitious plans, but the Edwards were ambitious men and their goals could not be achieved by timidity and inaction.

As noted earlier, an important component of the English strategy was Gascon support. Not only did Aquitaine's loyalty to Edward have to be beyond question so that he would not fear it abandoning him while the Black Prince mounted his next campaign to the north, but he needed the men and money of Aquitaine to make that campaign possible. Shortly after the prince arrived in Bordeaux he assembled the local lords and bade them pledge their support. His words to them at this point are essential in understanding the purpose of the actions that followed, culminating in the battle of Poitiers.

> He informed them that he […] intended, on behalf of his father, to demand the realm of France as his right and his heritage. On these points, he asked their counsel; many of them advised him to meet the king of France in arms. Hearing this, the prince told them that he could not do so without their help, in arms as well as in goods […] Immediately without contradiction [tax revenue] was granted to him. And the prince assigned a day for everyone who was willing to go and stand with him; and those who were not ready to come with him on that day, he would not consider his loyal friends.[90]

The Black Prince began marshalling his troops in La Reole, and then moved to Bergerac two weeks later to officially launch his campaign. It was not as numerous a force as his father had brought to Crécy, perhaps only 7,000 men, but they were all mounted and ready for battle. According to Froissart, the ratio of archers to knights was 3:1, demonstrating the English acknowledgement of the unique advantage of massed longbowmen.[91] By the Agincourt campaign of 1415, the ratio had increased to 5:1. Historian Clifford Rogers considers the available sources and is more inclined to rely upon the numbers provided by Burghersh, who reported a composition of 4,000 infantry (mostly men-at-arms) and 2,000 archers.[92] The prince ordered the Seneschal of Gascony, John de Chiverston, to remain behind with 2,000 men. Since the *chevauchée* of the previous year had not decisively engaged an army of either France or Armagnac, it had done nothing to safeguard Gascony from future incursions. Though he would later be criticized for dividing his forces, the prince had no choice but to leave a body of men for the protection of the Duchy.

On 4 August the *chevauchée* was underway. The invasion force moved swiftly northward, stopping every day or two to reprovision at the well-stocked larders of the towns of central France. The Anglo-Gascon forces wanted for nothing but opposition. The townspeople were surely well-informed of the campaigns of the autumn and winter of 1355–1356, but they had no army with which to oppose the Black Prince. Much like the advance through Normandy during the Crécy campaign of the previous decade, of which many of the English invaders were veterans, little time was spent investing fortifications. The prince was seeking battle; he did not wish to subject himself to strategic consumption, reducing his numbers in order to garrison strongpoints that he had no need to man. He maintained the integrity of his force, ever remaining focused upon the battle that Jean would surely offer. If the French king shrank again from a direct confrontation, could there be any question that he was unfit to sit on the throne?

Jean was finally taking concrete actions to assemble an army capable (or so he thought) of repulsing the *chevauchée*. He was, as has been discussed, sorely wanting for money, even before the devastation of the previous twelve months' campaigns. The French king made efforts to raise money through taxation and coin devaluation. These efforts, however, were unresponsive, insufficient, and above all, highly unpopular. English propagandists would use these examples of Valois fiscal ineptitude to increase the attractiveness of a Plantagenet ruler on the throne, promising economic stability and lower taxes. Despite Jean's monetary woes, men eager to fight the English were rallying at the rendezvous points north of the River Loire.

If the king's intelligence network could not provide him with the exact composition of the Black Prince's army, it could hardly have been difficult to detect the swath of devastated land that was at times nearly 50 miles wide.[93] There were probably masses of refugees flooding the countryside, but considering the speed with which the Anglo-Gascon horsemen advanced (nearly 200 miles in only twenty-four days), those who escaped the fire and sword would not have been able to keep ahead of the prince's progress. His target must have been as clear to Jean as it was unbelievable. Vierzon, on the Cher, was almost exactly two-thirds of the way along a direct route from Bergerac to Paris.

Historian H.J. Hewitt notes that when the prince crossed the River Cher on 28 August, 'the nature of the *chevauchée* underwent a change. The routine devastation along the route of march was now accompanied by military actions against objectives remote from the route of the main force.'[94] However, Hewitt does not explain *why* the nature changed; he dismisses it. The prince had been conducting this invasion for three and a half weeks and was growing restless for battle. Froissart writes that the English 'had found the country of Auvergne, which they had entered and overrun, very rich, and all things in great abundance; but they would not stop there, as they were desirous of combating their enemies'.[95] In fact, he had left England over a year before, and had been on campaign for nearly the entire time with only short breaks. Additionally, the young prince was well aware that the longer it took to bring his father's enemy to battle, the more time the French would have to prepare. The closer he got to Paris, the more men he would have to face. When Edward III had approached the outskirts of Paris in 1346, he found that his options for selecting the most advantageous battlegrounds had been greatly reduced. Now finding himself in a similar situation, the prince recognized that once he crossed the Loire, he would be on the very doorstep of Paris, in the heart of Valois support, and with a river behind him blocking the option of retreat should it prove necessary. By drawing Jean south of the Loire, the prince could maintain his lines of communication and lines of retreat towards the safety of the Gascon frontier. Such a move would also make the French king stretch out his own formations, away from their logistical stores. Therefore the Black Prince made the critical decision to adjust the manner in which he was conducting his *chevauchée*. He did not want to repeat the success of the raids of 1355; he wanted to improve upon it.

Romorantin

Seated in Paris, Jean II's plan for defeating the Black Prince had two main components. Both relied upon the inflow of great numbers of troops. As his men arrived, Jean's chief concern was of course to build his army, uniting one force of tremendous numerical advantage over the English raiding party. However, since he could not simply wait for the Black Prince to attack him, and he had no way of predicting the next target of the *chevauchée*, Jean also sent large forces – oftentimes numbering hundreds of men-at-arms – out to reinforce the garrisons throughout the regions vulnerable to attack, including Anjou, Poitou, Maine and Touraine. By 28 August 1356, Jean had moved his rallied forces to Chartres, an ancient city pre-dating Roman occupation, only 60 miles south-west of Paris. Just as the Black Prince had done before leaving his own base of operations at Bordeaux earlier in the summer, Jean issued a summons to his nobles that carried with it a threat: no knight who wished to be considered loyal to the crown could ignore this call to arms. On the same day that Jean was arriving at Chartres, the English army reached Vierzon along the River Cher. This town boasted a strong but poorly defended castle and held great quantities of food and wine, from which the English replenished their stores. Froissart reports that the invaders numbered 2,000 men-at-arms and 6,000 archers. Jean's army was nearer to 8,000 men-at-arms, with many hobelars besides. Each army thus ended the month of August less than 50 miles on either side of Orléans.

Orléans, the largest city in the region, sat on the River Loire, which the Black Prince would have to cross in order to effect the link-up with his reinforcements to the north. The prince had had little difficulty crossing the first major river along his route, the Garonne, but recent rains had swollen the waters of the Loire, leaving fords impossible to find. There were, of course, ample bridges across the river, but all of them that had existed between the major towns had been ordered destroyed by the French king. The ones that remained, for surely Jean would not unnecessarily restrict his own manoeuvrability, crossed amid heavily fortified towns and were thus denied to the English army. Constant reports were coming back to the French king, so he knew that he was closing in on the invader, but he still did not know precisely where he should direct his main army.

To determine the English army's exact size, disposition and location, Jean dispatched 200 men-at-arms, under the lead of Grismouton de Chambly. This knight was completely unsuccessful at either locating the prince's main body or at reporting any information to his king. English scouts engaged the French reconnaissance party and captured or killed enough of them so that no survivors were able to return to their own camp with news of the English. The victory had two effects on the Black Prince as he further developed his course of action. First, it likely led him to believe, rightfully, that Jean was largely ignorant of his precise strength and location. Second, it would have encouraged him to take full advantage of his campaign's growing momentum by following up this most recent success. To do so he would have to move quickly against a known target. Were he to merely continue his advance he would surely encounter additional French forces, but he was not seeking more chance engagements; he yearned for another Crécy, at which he had 'earned his spurs' and his legendary sobriquet. This time, however, with the additional English forces under the Duke of Lancaster threatening the north of France, they together could gain a truly decisive victory and end this war that had already raged for nearly twenty years.

The Black Prince continued his march along the River Cher, approaching the great town of Tours, at which he hoped to cross the Loire. Lancaster, meanwhile, led his much smaller army south along the River Mayenne, to the city of Angers, 60 miles west of Tours along the Loire. Le Baker reports that for one night the two English armies could see each other's campfires across the river, but that neither could effect the link-up. Unable to cross at Angers, he turned back towards the coast and successfully besieged the Breton city of Rennes. While it is widely recognized that Lancaster and the prince had some sense of a plan to converge against Jean's army, here can be detected another indicator that neither commander considered the link-up a necessary component of King Edward's strategy. Historian Michael Prestwich, an advocate of medieval generalship, writes on this point:

> It can be argued that the movements of the armies in 1356 was not predetermined by a calculated strategy, but although there is no documented plan of campaign, it is impossible to believe that the

attempted junction of forces at the Loire was not part of an ambitious, deliberate and calculated series of moves.[96]

Had there existed a definite plan to unite the two armies, Lancaster would have taken a different course of action. In order to keep pressure on Jean, he should have advanced east along the north shore of the Loire. Perhaps he could have crossed at Saumur, 30 miles to the east of Angers, as one component of Jean's forces eventually did, or he could have continued as far as Tours. The *Anonimalle Chronicle*, written nearly twenty-five years after the campaign, claims that Lancaster did march to the walls of Tours, but then turned back because he could not cross there. There is, however, no other record of his having advanced this far.

The most probable cause for Lancaster to abandon his eastward advance was that he would not have wanted to face Jean's army without the added numbers of the Black Prince. But it is also clear that he had confidence in the prince and his men to act independently. The march to Rennes from Angers took him more than 60 miles farther from the prince's forces. Any hope of either uniting the armies or attacking Jean from two different directions was gone. Lancaster could have endeavoured by his march to draw off some of Jean's forces and thus increase the prince's odds against him, but this alternative is not likely. The goal of the entire campaign was to compel the French king to commit to a decisive battle, and this could best be accomplished by lulling him into a sense of complacency due to a trust in his overwhelming numbers. Had the Black Prince been able to add Lancaster's numbers to his own, Jean may have refused battle even longer than he already did against the divided force.

One of the last obstacles that remained between the prince and the battle he sought was the fortified town of Romorantin. With any luck, Jean would consider Romorantin a town worth defending, and would march to raise the prince's siege. On 31 August the English moved quickly against the town, where they once again ran into a French scouting party, this time headed by the Lords of Craon and Boucicault. The invaders swept the defenders through the town, forcing them to blockade themselves in the castle. The Black Prince spent the night in the town, but with his characteristic sense of urgency, began besieging the castle the next morning. He had organized his army for speed and battle, not for conducting siege warfare, so the English had no siege engines with them to batter down the walls. His men did use ladders to attempt to scale the castle walls, and also set fire to the great wooden doors. Retreating from this assault, the two French lords barricaded themselves in the castle's keep. Now the Black Prince had a decision to make that would have tremendous impact on the entire campaign. The course of action that he decided upon reveals much about the prince's motives for his conduct of this phase of the war. While he did have some loose designs of linking up with his father and the Duke of Lancaster somewhere in central or northern France, probably in the neighbourhood of Tours, it would be incorrect to assume that the Black Prince did not welcome the opportunity to defeat 'the Usurper' on his own. The prince was supremely confident in his army, in himself as its commander, and in his very cause against the French. He had not tasted defeat since he set foot on the Continent. After Crécy, supporters had rallied behind his father. Now, after his own fabulously profitable raid in 1355, he had no shortage of enthusiastic recruits for this, his latest enterprise.

Positioned before the walls of Romorantin, with the French host a mere 30 miles away, he decided to make a stand. In addition to the strategic reasons for assaulting this strongpoint, the Black Prince was of the breed of men who favour action. He undoubtedly would have seconded the advice offered by some like-minded French knights later in the war, who suggested: 'You are seeking for adventures, and when they fall into your mouth, take advantage of them, for by all means allowed by the laws of arms, every man ought to molest his enemy.'[97] The two nobles trapped in the tower presented an opportunity he did not wish to ignore. Either he would capture them or he would draw Jean into battle when he came to relieve the siege. The Black Prince would, in either case, accomplish a desirable end. He knew that the keep could likely hold out for far more than the two days that it would take Jean's army to march to its relief. He also knew that the French king had no choice but to make that march. Jean had spent much time and expense raising an army with which to repulse the invader. He may have been able to justify avoiding battle to this point, but now the prince was weighed down with heavy booty collected from French subjects and he was sitting, tauntingly, within the reach of the king. Jean's reputation could not afford to allow the English ravagers to roam the countryside unchecked indefinitely.

Unwilling to order a reckless assault against the strong keep, and never one to waste time in an endeavour, the Black Prince ordered the construction of siege weapons. In addition to stone-throwing machines, sappers went to work burrowing under the keep's walls. Thus, while English stones ripped the roof off from above, tunnels set alight weakened the walls from below. The defenders within must have felt as sure as their besieger that the French king would arrive with his army and relieve them, for they had no hope of resisting unaided. Craon and Boucicault would certainly have known of Jean's proximity, and of the relative strength of the two armies, and thus would have been anxious but hopeful. On the third day of the siege they would have been expectant, on the fourth and fifth, increasingly despondent. Awakening on the sixth day from what could not have been a restful sleep, the two lords knew that no help was coming. On 3 September they surrendered what was left of their garrison and the Black Prince occupied the keep.

Victory at Poitiers

Soon after, the Black Prince learned that he would presently have the battle he so eagerly sought. Though Jean had not come to relieve the besieged Romorantin, he had advanced his army from Orléans to Tours, a distance of 60 miles. Now less than four days' march away, the reticent king appeared willing to face the English in combat. It remained only for the Black Prince to select defensible ground for the battle.

Romorantin to Poitiers

The prince, undaunted by his inability to merge with Lancaster's army, but not yet having found his choice of defensible ground, advanced west towards Tours, ravaged the region to its south, and thus drew Jean closer to battle. Chandos' Herald tells us that the French king found it increasingly difficult to ignore the incursion: 'Then it is very certain that the news reached King John, who was greatly moved, and said that he should lightly esteem himself, if he took not great vengeance.'[98] Jean, for his part, continued his advance towards the English invaders. The French host swelled as it moved. It contained not only French, but also Scottish, German and Castilian soldiers. While not the multinational force that Philip had amassed to chase down Edward III at Crécy, it was a formidable assembly, nonetheless. Whereas neither English army had been able to cross the Loire, the river posed no such impediment to its sovereign. Jean divided his army and crossed the river at will via a string of river crossings, each a day's march from the next, at the friendly towns of Meung, Blois, Amboise and Tours.

The Black Prince stayed one move ahead of his French rival, but made no effort to outdistance his pursuer. True, the English were heavy-laden with their recently-acquired booty, but if the young prince feared capture, he did not abandon the slow wagons. Either he thought that he could outpace Jean, which he did not seem to be attempting to do, or he wanted the French army to catch him – at a place of his choosing. The only other possibility is that he was ignorant of the pursuit. Certainly he did not have accurate information regarding the French army's whereabouts, but there is no doubt that he knew they were on the move. On the night of 11 September, with Jean close on his heels, the prince camped at Montbazon. Here a papal representative, the Cardinal of Périgord, attempted to offer terms, but the impetuous prince would not hear them.

This stage of the English invasion often puzzles historians. Why would the prince not treat with the envoy? But few likely possibilities exist. The first, that he believed it to be a ruse intended to delay him until Jean could close a trap around him is unlikely. As already shown, the English prince was in no hurry to return to Bordeaux. With the French king steadily closing in on him, he tarried two days more, 15–16 September, at Châtellerault, during which time the French bypassed the enemy army to encamp first at Chauvigny, and then at a position closer to Poitiers. While the prince's delay at Châtellerault is often questioned, few have criticized the French failure to attack him at this opportunity. Jean certainly could have caught him during his stay at Châtellerault, but was probably endeavouring to manoeuvre to ground more of his own choosing. If this is the case, it grants us perspective on each commander's intentions as the seemingly inevitable battle neared. Jean, clearly, did not yet wish to engage the English forces, and one can safely assume that he had made this decision based upon his fundamental strategy of refusing to give battle on the Black Prince's terms. He had seen the effects of such an error, and would not make the same mistake as his father. It is not enough to explain his circumnavigation of the English position by arguing that he was trying to cut off the invaders' retreat, because they had stopped, and were well within his reach. He had adequate forces to manoeuvre a significant part of them to the prince's rear to prevent his escape. No, Jean was continuing his practice of avoiding battle until he could be satisfied that an overwhelming victory was his to win.

As for the Black Prince, he could have been doing little else than inviting an attack by Jean on ground that favoured the English. The Black Prince, at the very least, was willing to risk a battle at this juncture; more likely, he was inviting one.

The Battle of Poitiers

⸺⸱•(•)•⸱⸺

Friday, 16 September

On Friday morning, King Jean, still in eager pursuit of what he considered a fleeing Anglo-Gascon army, hurriedly crossed the River Vienne at the Chauvigny bridge, less than 15 miles due east of Poitiers. Froissart alludes to the building tension of the chase, noting that Jean 'was afraid the prince might escape him, a thing he was most anxious to prevent'.[99] Prince Edward, who had camped along the east bank of the river two days earlier at Châtellerault, 20 miles to the north, was unaware that the French had made such rapid progress. When his scouts came back later that day and reported to him on the French position, the prince was surprised but not discomfited. He had been waiting for Jean to bring battle. There was no other reason for him to have prolonged his stay in the area. It certainly was not a good area to rest his men, for they 'found great difficulty in procuring forage, with the result that the army suffered a serious lack of provisions'.[100] Thus, it becomes apparent that the Black Prince was determined to fight Jean, even to the point that he was willing to sacrifice his own logistical preparedness in order to tarry long enough to let the French catch up with his army and offer battle.

Professor Clifford Rogers discusses additional indicators that the English actually desired to face the French in battle, noting that there were several alternatives that Prince Edward could have taken to avoid fighting the French, had that been his intention. The prince had, however, since 28 August when he had learned of Jean's pursuit, made decisions that made combat between the two armies more likely. His siege of Romorantin, movements against Tours, and his delay at Châtellerault all belie what one would expect of a commander in desperate flight. As Rogers explains, Jean was attempting 'to pin the English in place against a sea or an uncrossable river, so that they could be starved until they were forced to take the tactical offensive or to surrender. The trick to conducting a successful *chevauchée* was not to avoid battle, but to avoid a trap of that sort.'[101] Almost as important as avoiding such a trap was ensuring Jean believed that the English had in fact stumbled into one. As the Capetian and

Valois kings demonstrated with great regularity, they would not attack unless they felt sure of victory.

The final proof that the prince was seeking battle that day is his response to the news that the French were little more than a day's march to the south. Prince Edward himself explained his actions at Châtellerault in a letter he wrote to his supporters in London one month after the battle.

> So we went towards Châtellerault, where there was a crossing over the river Vienne and stayed there for four days to find out for certain what the king was doing. He came with his army to Chauvigny, 20 miles from us, to cross the same river towards Poitiers … [102]

H.J. Hewitt explains that at this point the Black Prince realized that 'it would be extremely difficult, if not impossible, to reach Bordeaux without a decisive battle and that the battle would have to be fought within a few hours. It was in fact imperative to press on further that very day, to snatch at the possibility of getting well south of Poitiers before the French army could deliver its blow.'[103] Hewitt was exactly right, or would have been, had his assumption been correct that the Black Prince was avoiding battle. Instead, rather than taking what was perhaps the prudent course, he set in motion his plan that very night to intercept the French army before they could complete their crossing of the river. He had the handlers of the English baggage trains spend Friday night crossing to the west bank of the Vienne. When morning came, they would be out of the way of their prince's army, which wanted nothing to impede its progress against the unsuspecting French forces a hard day's ride down the road.

Saturday, 17 September

> A quarter before dawn on Saturday, the prince sent for the earls of Warwick, Suffolk and Salisbury and for the other earls and lords and captains of his host and told them the news that he had heard of his enemies from his scouts; and immediately the said lords armed themselves and heard mass, devoutly kneeling and praying to God for aid and succour; and they had their armour laced up and they mounted their horses and crossed the bridge of Châtellerault. They left the highway to Poitiers and turned their path towards Chauvigny.[104]

Was this an army attempting to avoid battle? Now only 150 miles from Bordeaux, the Black Prince's army could have continued its march south-west, attempting to regain the lead over Jean's assembled host, but chose instead to attack. The *Scalachronica* reports that 'after the said Prince had spent all night at

The Battle of Poitiers

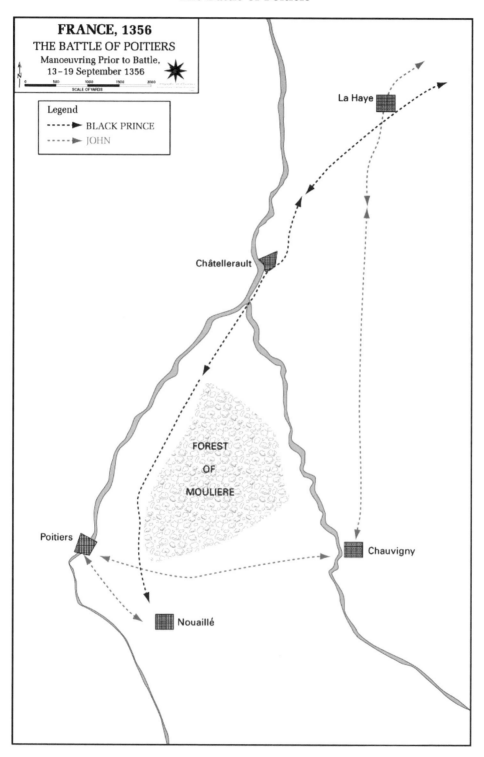

FRANCE, 1356
THE BATTLE OF POITIERS
Manoeuvring Prior to Battle,
13–19 September 1356

SCALE OF YARDS
0 500 1000 1500 2000

Legend
BLACK PRINCE
JOHN

La Haye

Châtellerault

FOREST

OF

MOULIERE

Poitiers

Chauvigny

Nouaillé

the castle Arraud-le-Sumail, he marched in great haste in his three columns in order of battle across country, intending to intercept the king of France's passage of the said river at the bridge of Chauvigny; but long before he could reach the said place, he perceived that the king had crossed.'[105] Jean still believed that the prince was further to the south. He, like so many historians since, believed that the Black Prince did not wish to fight, in which case the Plantagenet would have continued his march towards the safety of the Gascon frontier with all possible haste. But he had grander plans for this campaign than he had had even for the *chevauchée* of the previous year.

The prince sent a strong reconnaissance party forward to scout the exact disposition of the French. Froissart tells us that the troop comprised sixty men-at-arms, including Sir Eustace d'Aubrecicourt and Sir Jean de Ghistelles.[106] Neither commander knew the other's whereabouts. Jean's army, itself trying to intercept the Black Prince along his southward route, marched west along the road to Poitiers. The English scouts encountered the rearguard of the fast-moving French army just west of Savigny-Lévescault, perhaps very near the fields on which the great battle would shortly be fought. According to Froissart, d'Aubrecicourt and his companions met a much larger force of French knights, and retreated on the English main body, which had stopped by a forest near Savigny-Lévescault.[107] A chase ensued. The 200 French pursuers then encountered the Black Prince's full force and, though they fought valiantly, were killed or captured almost to the man. Le Baker, the *Anonimalle Chronicle* and the *Scalachronica* each differ greatly from Froissart on the description of events, chiefly due to the details they each omit. The various other depictions seem to portray the event described by Froissart, because of the common list of captured French knights, which in each case includes the Comte de Joigny.[108] Of the four descriptions, only Froissart mentions the English scouting party. His account of events provides further confusion by including a story of a second English reconnaissance. If it were not for the fact that the account of the earlier scout mission had included the capture of the French counts, this second tale might almost match the other sources better than did the first.

In Froissart's telling of the second reconnaissance patrol, after selecting the site on which the battle would be fought and beginning preparations for the French attack:

> The prince sent out the Captal de Buch, Sir Aymenon Pommiers, Sir Barthélemy de Burghersh, and Sir Eustace d'Aubrecicourt to learn the position of the French army, and with them two hundred men-at-arms, all mounted on the finest chargers. They rode so well, searching all sides, that they gained exact information concerning the French camp, which was bristling with armed men. These scouts could not refrain from harassing

the rear of the French; some they unhorsed and took prisoner, at which the army began to take alarm. News of this reached the king of France as he was about to enter the city of Poitiers.[109]

This episode could possibly have occurred according to Froissart's description, but it is more likely a blending of the activities of the earlier patrol, and of a later reconnaissance that the Black Prince ordered, even if it is nowhere else mentioned.

The Black Prince, in his version of events contained in the letter to the Londoners, confirms the description given by the first three chroniclers:

> And on hearing [that King Jean had crossed ahead of us] we decided to hasten towards him on the road which he would have taken in order to fight him. But his battalions had already passed when we got to the place where we expected to meet him, and only part of his army, some seven hundred men-at-arms, fought us. We captured the counts of Auxerre and Joigny and the Lord of Castillon and many others were taken or killed on both sides … [110]

It could be argued that any account written by the Black Prince to his subjects after the great victory at Poitiers would paint the most valorous picture of him in any circumstance. It is true that it is difficult to find a negative depiction of him in any source. But the fact that he may have spun (and probably did spin to some extent) his telling of the course of events to describe his decisions and actions in a more favourable light does not mean that the basic facts of his account are untrue. If one allows for the possibility that the Black Prince was intentionally venturing deep into Jean's territory, seeking out decisive battle with the French king, it would follow naturally that when he identified an opportunity to have such a battle, he would seize it. Even if he had not adopted such an ambitious strategy – if the Black Prince merely happened to learn that the king's army had overshot his own as it crossed the Vienne – it should be acknowledged that from what we know of the prince's disposition, he would likely have seized upon his chance to strike his opponent in the rear and do him injury, rather than just fly south, particularly if the best route to Bordeaux was blocked by Jean, who had unwittingly passed him at Chauvigny. The Black Prince in this instance then was exercising *prudence* by exploiting his brief period of local numerical superiority as he attacked Jean's rearguard.

We must add one last point to our discussion of the encounter on the seventeenth; the *Anonimalle Chronicle* claims that King Jean was present and that he afterwards retreated to the hill south-east of Poitiers, where he would remain until the battle. It is more likely that Jean was already heading towards Poitiers, still attempting to catch up with the Black Prince whom he assumed to be to his front. When the French king heard of the action against his rearguard, he halted his march and prepared for the battle he had so eagerly anticipated. This course of action is in concert with the record of events for Saturday night and Sunday morning in all four of the accounts. Le Baker proposes this sequence of events exactly, and the other three each match almost word for word that the prince spent Saturday night in a wood near that day's fight, and that he marched towards Poitiers the next morning, where he knew the French army to be arrayed.[111]

Sunday, 18 September

The English army had another early day on Sunday, but, while eventful, it would prove to be largely free of fighting. By most accounts the Black Prince advanced his army nearer to Jean's position, which he knew to be on the elevated plains south-east of the city of Poitiers. Froissart alone has this march occur on Saturday afternoon.[112] The action on Sunday, however, centred around ongoing negotiations between the two armies, facilitated by a papal delegation. At first the cardinals rode back and forth between the two commanders, but at some point, probably mid-afternoon, the king and the prince agreed to a day-long truce and representatives from each army met between the two positions to discuss terms of peace.[113] Chandos' Herald provides the most detailed account of the meeting, listing among the participants the Count of Tancarville, the Archbishops of Sens and Taurus, and the Lords Charny, Bouciquaut and Clermont from the French side; and, representing the English, Warwick, Suffolk, Burghersh, Audley and Chandos. Charny suggested to have the contest resolved by 100 champions from each army, but Warwick refused any reconciliation but by battle and led the prince's representatives back to the English lines.[114] There Prince Edward, and, presumably Salisbury and Oxford, were seeing to the defences. Edward had selected defensible ground but knew from experience that it could be improved to increase his advantage.

The Black Prince was not the only medieval commander capable of adapting his tactical plan according to lessons learned from past encounters. King Jean, as he prepared to take the field at Poitiers, had with him the veteran Scot, William Douglas, who had been a key player at the battle of Neville's Cross. John of Fordun submits that 'he brought with him a great many Scots, strong in body, accomplished in arms, and learned in warfare'.[115] It was at William's recommendation that Jean dismounted so many of his men for the coming battle. The few hundred horsemen that he did employ, Geoffrey le Baker reports, the French king ensured were properly outfitted with heavy mail to protect them from the arrows of the English longbowmen.[116] Confident of the sufficiency of this measure, Jean even instructed them to target the English archers. Le Baker records Jean's order to his mounted knights to 'attack the archers at the beginning of the battle, and to trample them underfoot with the spurs of their horses'.[117] This reference demonstrates that at least some of the French commanders possessed an understanding of preferred English battle tactics, and was surely a response to the devastatingly costly lesson that Philip VI and all with him had learned only ten years before at Crécy. We would be remiss to take the line so often argued that the French learned nothing between the two battles, or, for that matter, between Poitiers and Agincourt. Not only did Jean attempt this remedy to a shortcoming he had identified in the earlier battle, but as we shall see, it proved particularly effective, and even forced the English to make a bold adjustment to their own plan to compensate for it. In any case, Black Prince biographer Henry Sedgwick was being unfair and perhaps a bit melodramatic when he put forth his assessment that 'this French army was very similar to that at Crécy, a mob of gentlemen who fought with brilliant valour and dazzling stupidity'.[118]

There exists little disagreement between historians over whether the French king desired battle. He had assembled a large army at great expense, and had already lost a tremendous amount of future income due to the Black Prince's despoiling of his lands in Berry, Anjou and Touraine. In addition to these fiscal considerations, and no less weighty on Jean's mind, was the degree to which his reputation had already suffered. Not only did he have his own diminished status to avenge, but also that of the French crown itself, tarnished in the previous decade by the triple loss at Sluys, Crécy and Calais. Now, with the Black Prince well within his grasp, Jean could not afford to let him slip away. After a half-hearted attempt at a peace conference on 18 September, Chandos' Herald reports the king to have exclaimed: 'Fair sirs, by my troth, you will so keep me back, I ween, that the prince will escape me. That Cardinal has certainly betrayed me, who made me abide here so long.'[119] A sentiment he followed with the distinctly menacing orders: 'See to it, if you find the English, that you engage in battle with them and spare not to put them all to death.'[120] Not only was this verbal order issued, but Jean gave the unmistakable sign that the French were to take no prisoners. He had Sir Geoffrey de Charny raise the *oriflamme*, described by Henry Knighton as: 'the scarlet standard, which is the token of Death'.[121] Chronicler Geoffrey le Baker confirms Jean's mood, reporting that 'the French leader in no way wanted peace, except by the fury of war'.[122] And Jean de Venette adds that 'pride reigned, confidence in the might and multitude of armed men persisted, and as a result a pitched battle was agreed upon. King [Jean] came to battle in high spirits.'[123] Froissart notes that Jean was 'impatient to fight the English'.[124]

The Black Prince, for his part, also wanted to engage in a decisive battle, though this point is very divisive among historians of the Hundred Years War.

Victory at Poitiers

Despite being outnumbered, he had apt reason to feel confident in the assuredness of his own victory. He had tasted nothing but success since reaching Bordeaux over a year before. Though the River Loire had thwarted his intended link-up with Lancaster, and the occasional fortification had resisted his assaults, these inconveniences were no deterrence from his ultimate goal: battle with the king of France, usurper of his father's title and the prince's own birthright. The English had faced and triumphed over greater odds at Crécy, and the prince's men were now seasoned veterans. There is little reason to believe Chandos' Herald's claim that on Monday morning 'the prince broke up camp; he began to ride, for that day he thought not to have battle, I assure you, but weened ever, most certainly, to continue to avoid the battle'.[125] John of Fordun, a Scottish chronicler in no way a fan of any English monarch, joins the herald in sowing doubt as to the prince's motives, writing:

> At last, the English Prince and his men, who were very few in comparison with the French, seeing that their position was shut in, had no hope of being able to escape; and being sore afraid of the numbers of those pitted against them, durst not, at first, openly come to blows with the French, who stood in their lines, and stirred not. So they planned a stratagem and shrew device, in order to part them asunder.[126]

Despite these accusations, there are indications that the Black Prince had taken measures to prepare for battle on the Maupertuis Plain. Sources record that the prince had ordered his men to dig ditches and other defensive structures as early as Saturday, and that they had continued to do so throughout the negotiation process that persisted all weekend. Froissart reports that 'In front [of their position] they dug several ditches, to prevent any sudden attack on horseback,' and le Baker adds that one reason the French were so confident of their victory was that the English 'were exhausted by their labours'.[127]

'The king, to prolong the matter and to put off the battle',[128] took his time and permitted the cardinals to make a show of actively pursuing peace negotiations between the two commanders. Jean felt assured of victory, and had nothing to lose by the postponement. Now, in addition to winning the battle, the French king would be able to say that he had repeatedly offered terms to the Black Prince, but that they had been at every turn rejected. Of course, Jean had not offered *reasonable* terms. Froissart writes that the Black Prince 'found the king of France so unbending that they would not stoop to making an agreement, unless they had four-fifths of the English knights as prisoners, and the prince and his men surrendered unconditionally – something they would never have done'.[129] Prince Edward, meanwhile, 'offered to give back to the king of France all towns and strongholds that he had captured on this expedition, to hand over all the prisoners that they had taken, and to swear not to take up arms against the king of France for seven years'.[130]

One may question why the prince offered such generous terms if he truly wanted to fight. There were, as there are for all decisions, several contributing factors. First, the prince, like Jean, wished to appear to show Christian restraint and avoid unnecessary violence if possible. To this end, Chandos' Herald reports that Prince Edward did not want to negotiate, 'but to avert the damage and sin of death [he would] agree to it'.[131] Froissart indicates that the cardinal praised the prince's wisdom.[132] Geoffrey le Baker is more elaborative:

> a certain cardinal Périgord came to the prince, and adjured him out of respect for God who died on the Cross and for the love of His mother the Virgin, and out of reverence for holy Church and in order to save the shedding of Christian blood, to suspend action for as long as was needed in order to open peace negotiations, promising future honour from his intervention if he was indeed allowed to intervene. The prince, in no way terrified by the usurper [Jean], neither feared battle nor turned away peace; but he modestly agreed to his holy father's request.[133]

Another point to consider is whether Prince Edward's offer was as generous as at it first seemed. It was not, and this is part of the reason Jean dismissed it. The damage the Anglo-Gascon army had already done to Jean's kingdom and to his reputation was a sufficient prize for the campaign, and even if the prince had had to surrender some of the material gains, his honour would remain intact.

The most important reason for offering terms, however, as explained by Froissart, reveals a great deal to the careful reader about the Black Prince's tactical shrewdness. Froissart suggests that the reason for the English attempt at negotiations was due to the fact that 'the English were afraid that the French might block them in their present position without making any attack'.[134] How should this be understood? Taken at face value, it merely implies that the English did not wish to be starved into submission. But Jean could not force a standstill by refusing to attack, because in battle either force can attack, however unwise the decision to do so may be. The French king could not prevent the prince from assuming the offensive. Attacking was always an option, but the Black Prince understood that it was a poor option. He appreciated the value of the tactical defence, and his plan demanded that he exploit it. He knew that by defending on well-selected and well-prepared ground he could defeat Jean's more than two-to-one advantage in numbers. By the same token, he knew that in his current situation he could not hope to succeed were he to assume the tactical offence.

Victory at Poitiers

Jean, however, was accommodating. He undoubtedly wanted to fight the Black Prince but had ridden very hard in order to have 'outstripped the prince',[135] and would necessarily have some of his dismounted forces straggling behind. Not wishing to repeat the mistakes of the overeager knights at Crécy, the French king waited. He also knew that time was on his side, because 'supplies were now so short in the prince's army that he either had to come to battle, or shamefully turn his back upon the enemy'.[136] Froissart echoes the urgency of the English logistical situation, saying that the prince's men 'were beginning to feel great want of stores, which was a cause of great concern to them'.[137] The French, however, being in their own territory, 'were provided with all kinds of supplies'.[138] Additionally, as would be expected, reinforcements continued to stream into the French camp. Le Baker reports that throughout the attempts at negotiations that occurred all day on Sunday, 'the French army increased by a thousand men-at-arms and many more common people'.[139] The *Scalachronica* goes so far as to claim that the cardinals 'acted for [the French] advantage [...] to prolong the affair to the detriment of the said Prince, [who should] run short of provisions and other munition, while their forces [the French] should be increased [by reinforcements] continually arriving'.[140] The *Eulogium historiarum* confirms the Black Prince's appraisal of his situation:

> But the prince, seeing the enemy was daily becoming stronger, preferred rather to engage than thus to prolong the matter to his own loss. For he often perceived now 200, now 300, now 500 Frenchmen hurrying by companies to the French column, a sight which worried him considerably.[141]

The various chronicles that describe the battle of Poitiers disagree on many points. One of the first and most basic of these debates concerns the organization of French forces and the number of divisions. As we have seen, it was common medieval practice to divide an army into three divisions, with the overall commander (often the king) commanding the third, or reserve. Edward III had done this during the Crécy campaign, the Scottish forces had done so at Neville's Cross, both armies had at Halidon Hill,[142] and, as we shall see the Black Prince followed this practice at Poitiers, though there he commanded the second division – the main body, as had the Archbishop at Neville's Cross. It should be no surprise then if Jean were to divide his army into three divisions at Poitiers. Froissart, perhaps the most cited of the chroniclers, reports that Jean did exactly this:

> On the advice of the constable [Gautier de Brienne, the Duke of Athens] and the marshals of France [Clermont and d'Audrehem], the army was drawn up in three great battalions [...] the first was under the command of

the Duc d'Orleans [Jean's brother, Philippe] [...] the second was commanded by the Duke of Normandy and his two brothers, Louis and Jean [Jean's three oldest sons]; the third by the king himself.[143]

This organization, however, omits the vanguard, commanded by the constable and the marshals, though Froissart frequently refers to 'the battalion of the marshals' as being independent of the three divisions.[144] The *Anonimalle Chronicle* likewise refers to the constable and marshals commanding the vanguard, and the Dauphin, the Duke of Orléans, and the French king each commanding a division.[145] Chandos' anonymous Herald, a more reliable source than Froissart, assigns the same leadership roles as Froissart, but refers to the units as four divisions.[146] John Capgrave's *Chronicle of England*, written perhaps sixty years after the event, also described the French army as being divided into four parts.[147]

Other sources, however, disagree. *Chronique des quatre premiers Valois* reverses the commanders of the second and third division.[148] The chronicler Henry Knighton reports that the French marshals commanded the first division, the Dauphin and the Duke of Orléans the second jointly, and Jean the third.[149] One might consider that his account agrees with le Baker, who curiously does not mention the Duke of Orléans at all in his listing of the commanders.[150] A reason for this omission may have been the nature of the French advance. As shall be discussed, the marshals' initial assault and that of the king at the end of the battle are each clearly discernible. Events during the heat of the battle, however, likely became difficult to distinguish with certainty, and contemporaries' errors in exact descriptions of the waves of the attack may be forgiven.

Another means we have of inferring the organization of the French forces is to observe their English counterparts, whom they were preparing to meet in battle. Le Baker reports that the Black Prince had withheld from the fight a force of 'four hundred men under the prince's banner kept in reserve to meet the usurper [Jean] and his soldiers'.[151] There are a few points to consider about this remark. If the prince arrayed his forces in three divisions according to custom, and held an additional 400 men from his command as a reserve, specifically chosen to combat King Jean and his reserve, it would make sense that the size of the reserve forces would be comparable. Chandos' Herald numbers Jean's reserve at 'four hundred barded horses and four hundred knights upon them, picked men', including the French king, himself, and twenty-three knights bannerette, including three the herald mentions by name: Guichard d'Angle, the Lord of Aubigny and Eustace de Ribemont.[152] He does not give an exact count of the prince's reserve, but we may infer that they were among his choicest knights. Being 'under the prince's banner', they likely were several of his personal retainers. And though the herald does not specifically say so, we do know from elsewhere that they had not yet engaged in the fight. Sir James Audley, who had to this point been alongside the prince, when he saw Jean's division advance, reportedly made the following request of the Black Prince:

> 'Sire,' quoth he, 'I have vowed to God and promised and sworn that wherever I should see the banner of the king of France in power there I would set on the first, so I beseech you for God give me leave, for it is high time to join battle.'[153]

Thus, we gain confirmation of the intended role of the two reserves. Each sought to face the other in combat befitting the chivalrous knights present on each side. The French surely could have fielded a cavalry reserve much greater than that under the prince, but Jean and his trusted subordinates decided that about 400 was the appropriate number. That this matched the English reserve may not have been intentional, but it would not be surprising if it had been. Knights on each side declared during Sunday's negotiations a willingness to fight a battle of champions – the best 100 from each army – and if the day instead had to be decided by 800 knights rather than 200, it would only attest to the gravity of the engagement and enhance the glory to be gained.

Whatever Jean had intended at the outset of the battle, it is clear that the French attacked in four waves, Jean leading the final one. What is most likely is that the two armies adopted the organization of troops that at the same time mirrored each other and followed historical precedent. It is natural that the two commanders would match the other division for division, even if there existed discrepancies in the size and composition of the divisions. Additionally, successful commanders of every historical era generally kept a small reserve of crack troops to be committed to the fight at the pivotal time and place, which could only be identified once the mêlée had begun. Thus, Jean divided his army into three divisions: the vanguard under the constable, the second division under his eldest son, and the third under his brother, the Duke of Orléans. The French king personally commanded the reserve. That it is often described as a division was, as it shall be seen, due to the fact that it had swollen to several times its original number as men from the broken divisions ahead of it flocked to the king's banner.

The vanguard itself was subdivided into three components. The constable led 4,000 dismounted infantrymen, an even mix of spearmen and crossbowmen,[154] as well as a battalion of mounted foreign troops from Jean's German allies.[155] Froissart passes down some of the names of the foreign horsemen, which he knew because men of the Black Prince's division captured all three of them during the rout of the first division: the Counts of Saarbruck, Nassau and Nido.[156] The two marshals each rode at the head of a mounted force with the mission of overrunning the longbowmen at the forefront of the English

The Battle of Poitiers

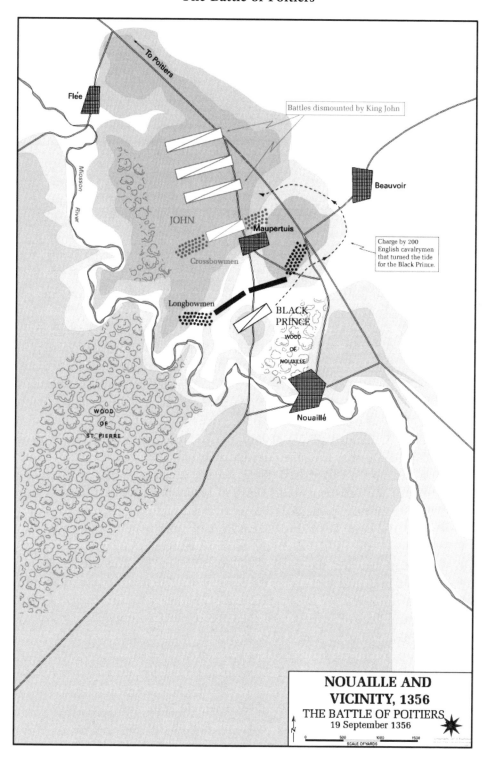

To Poitiers

Flée

Miosson River

Battles dismounted by King John

Beauvoir

JOHN

Maupertuis

Crossbowmen

Charge by 200
English cavalrymen
that turned the tide
for the Black Prince.

Longbowmen

BLACK
PRINCE

WOOD
OF
NOUAILLE

WOOD
OF
ST. PIERRE

Nouaillé

**NOUAILLE AND
VICINITY, 1356**
THE BATTLE OF POITIERS
19 September 1356

N

0   500   1000   1500
SCALE OF YARDS

formation.[157] Sir Thomas Gray, author of the *Scalachronica*, referred to these forces collectively as 'the advanced guard',[158] which is a fitting term, as it distinguishes it from the constable's units composed primarily of infantry or dismounted cavalry soldiers. The *Chronique des quatre premiers Valois* also lends support to this interpretation when it refers to 'the divisions of the marshals'.[159]

Jean's reserve was composed of approximately 400 distinguished knights. This should not be confused with the elect knights whom the marshals had chosen for special service at Jean's bequest: 'At his command the two marshals rode off, visiting each battalion in turn to make an impartial choice of three hundred knights and squires, the swiftest and the bravest of the whole army, all mounted on the finest chargers and armed from head to foot.'[160] These men were to disrupt the formations of longbowmen, thereby giving to the much larger divisions of dismounted men-at-arms, who were less adequately armoured, the time to cross the broad field and close with and defeat the English soldiers.[161] Positioned to their right as they faced south was the Dauphin's division. We can assume this with confidence because Chandos' Herald tells us that 'on one of the sides it took its place and covered a great space'.[162]

When the two armies met, the constable's force clashed with Warwick's and Salisbury's men, while the Dauphin met with the prince's division. It seems unlikely that the two French divisions would line up in one formation and then cross each other's advance as they neared the English position. Orléans' division was to the rear of the first two, probably behind the Dauphin. Jean remained with his picked reserve atop the ridge from which he could best view the battle as it unfolded. Such a plan of attack should indicate that the French had taken some lessons from their dearly purchased experience at Crécy.[163] This was not just another ill-advised charge against a strong defensive position. Hundreds of the best-armoured knights in France were selected for this key role that specifically addressed the great failing of the previous historic encounter. The other key improvement in the French plan of attack was the composition of the vanguard. At the previous meeting, dismounted Genoese crossbowmen had led the charge, followed closely by armoured knights. Neither had been effective against the mass of English longbowmen. The van at Poitiers accounted for this tactical error. The heavy cavalry charge would penetrate the lines of archers, and then the constable's dismounted infantry would exploit the gaps. Jean had a good plan that he must have been very confident in as he saw the marshals surge forward. But the Black Prince, too, had a plan that he believed would allow him to prevail over the force more than twice the strength of his own.

Having arrived on Sunday at the fields where the battle was to be fought, the Black Prince took advantage of the time that the cardinals spent in their attempts to negotiate a peace and prevent the combat from taking place.

The Battle of Poitiers

Appreciating the value of defensible terrain, he reconnoitred the ground that he found most suitable for his purposes. The spot the Black Prince selected was a field 900 metres wide, situated between two dense woods. His defensive line would face generally north, running along the crest of a minor ridge, and be tied into the wood on either side. At the centre of his intended position was a sharply descending southward-facing bowl with a swamp at its centre. The bowl is 300 metres wide and 300 metres long. Its bottom lies 17 metres below the highest point on its ridge, the north-east corner. Its grade averages 10 per cent, but reaches as high as 20 per cent on the steepest slope. The ground to his front was a gently undulating broad plain extending north for 4 miles to the walls of Poitiers. A ridge extended east–west half a mile to his front. Behind it the low ground was spacious enough to conceal a large army, and a quarter mile farther north rose the higher plain upon which sat Poitiers. Though other sources supply details that help explain exact dispositions and movements of the various forces on the field, le Baker provides the most detailed description of the ground the Black Prince chose.

> [The Black Prince] surveyed the scene and saw that to one side there was a nearby hill encircled by hedges and ditches outside but clear inside, for part of it was pasture and bramble-thickets, part of it planted with vines, and the rest sown fields. In these fields he believed the French army to be drawn up. Between our men and the hill was a broad deep valley and marsh, watered by a stream. The prince's battalion crossed the stream at a fairly narrow ford with their carts and leaving the valley, occupied the hill beyond the marshes and ditches, where they easily concealed their positions among the thickets, lying higher than the enemy. The field in which our vanguard and centre were stationed was separated from the level ground which the French army occupied by a long hedge and ditch, whose other end reached down to the marsh already mentioned. The Earl of Warwick, in command of the vanguard, held the slope down to the marsh. In the upper part of the hedge, well away from the slope, there was a certain open space or gap, made by the carters in autumn, a stone's throw away from which our rearguard was positioned, under the command of the Earl of Salisbury.[164]

This passage requires careful reading. It must first be recognized that the description begins with the Black Prince surveying the scene from the south bank of the River Miosson. After skirting the east border of the Maupertuis woods, he passed through the town of Maupertuis-Nouaillé, noting the 'castle', which was actually the formidable abbey that still stands today.[165] He had then crossed the river at the south-east corner of the wood, and proceeded onto the

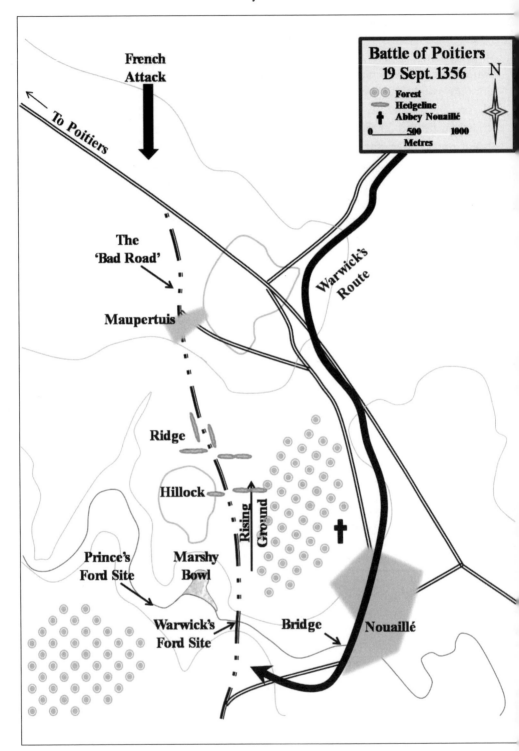

Battle of Poitiers
19 Sept. 1356

N

Forest
Hedgeline
Abbey Nouaillé

0   500   1000
Metres

French
Attack

To Poitiers

The
'Bad Road'

Warwick's
Route

Maupertuis

Ridge

Hillock

Rising Ground

Prince's
Ford Site

Marshy
Bowl

Warwick's
Ford Site

Bridge

Nouaillé

rising ground in which he would have Warwick establish his trains. As he looked north, he could see the hill to his front left, with the marsh between it and him. Once the prince recrossed the river at a ford west of the marshy bowl, he ascended the hill. It rose on both sides of the marsh. He, naturally, sought to position himself on the higher side, the better from which to command, so he occupied the hill to the left.

From the top he could see that the hilltop was naturally well-fortified by hedges, thickets and vines. To his front, across lower ground, the French were arrayed on level, sown fields. A 'bad road' – the Maupertuis – extended from the right of his position forward to Jean's army, which was now between him and the city of Poitiers, 4 miles to the north. He assigned the high ground to the east of the marsh, where the road passed it heading south to the river, to his vanguard under the Earl of Warwick. The road was lined on both sides by dense hedges. With Warwick's men-at-arms defending the 200 metres from the marsh to the road, the rearguard, under the Earl of Salisbury, would cover the remaining 200 metres between the road and the wood line. To the front of each, archers augmented the natural defences of the hedgerows by digging ditches, an activity Froissart reports the archers had begun as early as Saturday.[166] Any ditches they had dug on Saturday must necessarily have been defensive preparations of the camp that they erected after the action against the French rearguard at or near Savigny. The Black Prince indicates in his own report that after that fight 'we had to encamp there to reassemble our troops; and the next day we went straight in the direction of the king [who was] […] ready for battle in the fields about 4 miles from Poitiers'.[167] The *Anonimalle Chronicle* sites the prince's Saturday night camp 'in a wood on a little river near the site of the [French] defeat'.[168]

The Black Prince knew that Jean had already determined to attack him, so now all that was left was to array his forces. The English organization, unlike that of the French, is uncontested by historians. Nearly every contemporary record is the same: the Earl of Warwick commanded the van, the prince the main body, and the Earl of Salisbury the rearguard.[169]

Jean's reconnaissance element, which consisted of four knights led by Sir Eustace de Ribemont, reported that the English army was arrayed as a single unit.[170] The scouts' view of the English position would have been much obscured by the terrain on which they were situated. The preponderance of hedgerows and vineyards would have prevented a clear line of sight. Additionally, not all of the English forces were yet in place when the French viewed the position. Warwick had at least part of his men, those still mounted, escorting the baggage train safely south of the River Miosson. The rest of the first division was either among the hedges, or on the slope descending away from the French onlookers. Either way they would be imperceptible. Salisbury had not

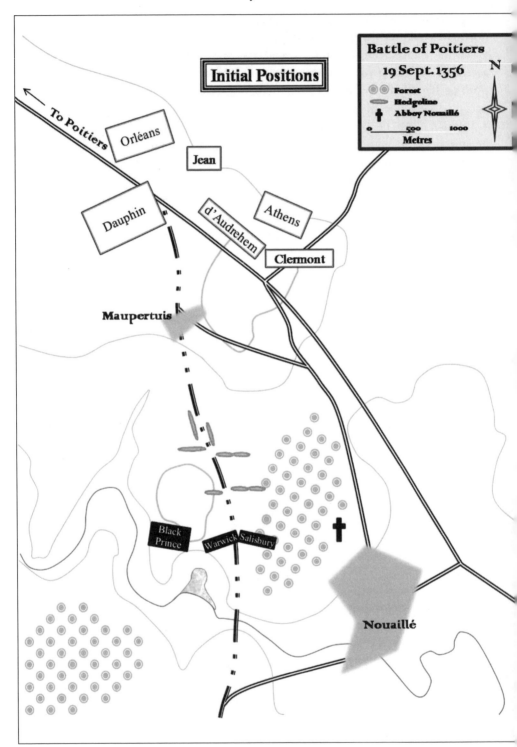

yet moved into position. Though the prince and his men were set, many of them were among the hedges and vines, or on the reverse slope of the hilltop they were occupying. Froissart, who offers the most detailed retelling of the French reconnaissance mission, reports that the most easily seen of the English soldiers were the archers, stationed forward of the men-at-arms who were only visible at the break in the hedge that would play such a central role in the first phase of the battle. The archers may have been especially visible if they were forward of their lines, digging ditches, as Froissart reports. The scouts rightly concluded that the defenders were 'most skilfully placed'.[171]

In addition to the three main battles, Froissart describes two forces, either of which may have been intended to serve as the English reserve. The first was 'a body of wise and brave knights [whom the Black Prince had ordered] to remain on horseback between his battalions, to withstand the battalion of the French marshals'.[172] Since the marshals were leading Jean's initial assault, this first mounted force was clearly not the reserve: it was intended to meet the French vanguard head-on. The second English troop also had a unique composition suited to their intended purpose: 'three hundred men and as many archers, all mounted, on a hill which was neither very high nor very steep, [who were] to move round under cover of this hill and strike at the Duke of Normandy's battalion which was drawn up on foot below it.'[173] The former of these two units was more likely the reserve, but as we shall see, it is all but impossible to know whether it had even formed before the French attacked, because of all the English forces only the main body under the Black Prince was in position when the battle began. The latter unit would be the right size and composition for the reserve, but more likely reflects the chronicler's mislabelled description of the Captal de Buch's flanking force, which was a hastily assembled troop that did not come into play until nearer the end of the battle.

If, at the end of the day on Sunday, Ribemont had been able to view the English position from above, he would have seen the main body arrayed according to the prince's plan, on the hilltop west of the marshy bowl. The archers and dismounted men-at-arms of Warwick's vanguard were also in position, preparing for the French onslaught.[174] The rearguard, under Salisbury, likely camped in or near the town of Nouaillé, east of the wood. Warwick's mounted contingent and the baggage trains spent the night there, as well. The archers and men-at-arms, however, occupied the ridge along the top of the marsh west of the woods, preparing their positions and guarding against French probes. It would not be unreasonable to believe the prince camped on or near the abbey grounds, especially since the cardinals had negotiated a truce for all of Sunday. One would expect that this suggestion is more logical than supposing the heir to the English throne slept in the vines and brambles among which he would mount his defence on Monday morning. The *Anonimalle Chronicle*, however, reports that 'the prince remained in the field all night'.[175] But Prince Edward was not digging ditches. Sir Thomas Gray tells us that 'negotiations were prolonged throughout the night'.[176] Whether the Black Prince slept in the field, at the abbey, or not at all that night, he was up very early Monday morning, and began his day in spiritual preparation for what now must have seemed an inevitable battle.

Monday, 19 September

It would be easy to imagine that the Anglo-Gascon lords would receive mass in the abbey, though it could just as likely have taken place in the field. There the cardinals tried one last time to secure a longer truce, but Jean, in particular, would wait no longer.[177]

On Monday morning, the prince and the great lords of the army with him heard mass in reverence of God, and then moved off towards Poitiers at dawn. And the Earl of Warwick crossed a narrow causeway over a marsh where he found a French town with a castle.[178]

Sunday's truce having expired, from the town of Nouaillé the Black Prince ordered Warwick to lead the baggage trains to the south bank of the Miosson. The English were already at a numerical disadvantage. They did not need to further diminish their numbers by placing a large guard on the great quantity of booty they had acquired during the *chevauchée*. The additional advantage of this position, the farthest from the French, was that it was also the closest to the road to English Bordeaux, and, importantly, already across the river. It has been argued that the prince did this so that he could retreat all the more easily.[179] While the prepositioning of the trains to the south of the Miosson would, of course, facilitate a retreat (and could a good commander be faulted for taking such a precaution?), it must not be forgotten that alternative courses of action were just as likely. We have already seen that when the Black Prince had prepared to cross the Vienne only a few days before, the first order he gave was for the trains to make the passage first, so that they would not be in the way of the armed troops when they needed to cross. The actions at the crossing of the Miosson at the Gué de l'Homme on Monday, 19 September, may appear reminiscent of this previous event, and in some ways they are, but a few key differences must be noted.

In the first case, at the Vienne, the English had been stationary and were preparing for a quick offensive strike against an enemy that had to that point escaped their detection. The French had advanced, searching out the Black Prince's army, which was then attempting to strike them in the rear. At the Miosson, the English had again been stationary, but they knew with a good deal of certainty the disposition of Jean's army, and many of the leaders had even spent the entire previous day in congress with them. Additionally, by the 19th, the Black Prince was preparing to make a defensive stand. He was merely

The Battle of Poitiers

positioning his baggage trains, a notoriously 'soft target', in a more secure location. It is overly presumptuous to assert that because he moved them further along the route towards Bordeaux that this meant he intended to retreat. After the battle, with King Jean and his youngest son in his possession, the prince headed south to the Gascon capital. So if Bordeaux were the prince's intended destination regardless of the outcome of the battle, one cannot assume that a movement in that direction is an indication that the Black Prince hoped to escape battle, no matter what Chandos' Herald might have inferred from his understanding of the tactical situation. Barber's assertion that 'there was no reason to move the baggage' unless 'he was attempting a cautious retreat'[180] is absurd. The baggage trains could only have served to complicate the prince's conduct of his defence had they remained among the defenders. Historical examples abound of the English positioning their trains to their rear during a battle, including Crécy, Verneuil and Agincourt, at which Henry V famously failed to provide adequate defence for them and consequently fell victim to a small French assault to his rear. The Black Prince, beginning this move at first light, was probably confident that Warwick would return before the impending battle began. He had only a few hundred metres to move, and even though the truce would expire less than two hours after sunrise,[181] the prince probably anticipated that there would be a long standoff before any actual fighting began, as was typical of medieval battles.[182]

Perhaps the most convincing sign that the English army was committed to fighting the battle at Poitiers that day is the composition of the forces that were escorting the baggage trains to the south bank of the Miosson. If that movement of the trains were truly the first stage of a retreat, who would be in the escort? One would expect that the entire vanguard under Warwick and Oxford would be accompanying the trains, with the prince's division following close behind and the Earl of Salisbury defending their rear. However, events on Monday morning did not resemble that supposition at all. The English army was drawn up ready for battle by dawn. Froissart attests to this, and Sir Thomas Gray reports that the Black Prince 'was ready in battle array'.[183] The archers and men-at-arms had spent the previous day digging and preparing their defences. These actions would not have been necessary for them to undertake unless they planned to fight there on Monday. Sunday had been a day of truce, so the threat was minimal, and they were very short on supplies, so these additional exertions would not only have been unwarranted, but detrimental to men about to attempt a 150-mile dash to safety. No, the Black Prince expected to fight on the Maupertuis Plain, and was making the necessary preparations for the battle.

There are several indicators that when Warwick crossed the Miosson he did not take his dismounted forces with him. First, there are the references to the fact that the prince's army was 'in battle array' at first light on Monday morning.

Victory at Poitiers

The men guarding the hedge and ditches would not have abandoned their posts to escort the baggage train unless the entire army was withdrawing. Warwick's dismounts were the front line of defence. No chronicler other than Chandos' Herald even hints that Warwick took his entire vanguard with him, but they all give evidence that they remained in place. Jean and his marshals could see the Black Prince's banners atop the small hill he was occupying. When he moved to the reverse slope of the hill, perhaps in an attempt to ascertain the progress of Warwick and the carts, the French marshals believed that the prince was retreating and so initiated the attack.[184] The prince would not have been with the forward-most of his forces. He had archers and men-at-arms positioned to his front, between himself and the French army. When the French marshals' mounted attack hit the English, the first forces they encountered were the English longbowmen, prepositioned among the hedges. From which division were these longbowmen? Rogers corrects Hewitt's mistaken assumption that the archers were from among the prince's division, so they must have come from either the vanguard or the rearguard.[185] These archers could have been Salisbury's men, and likely some of them were, but it is more probable they were from the van.

Le Baker, in describing the English array, tells us that 'the field in which our vanguard and centre were stationed was separated from the level ground which the French army occupied by a long hedge and ditch',[186] and also that 'the archers [were] positioned in safe trenches along the ditch and beyond the hedge'.[187] Therefore, these archers were Warwick's, since the men in this sector were from the 'vanguard and centre' and the centre had no archers. These men took the first defensive action of the battle. Jean, it must be remembered, had ordered the marshals' select troop of heavy cavalrymen to 'trample the archers underfoot' and the impetus for the marshals' attack was the fear that the prince was attempting to flee. When Clermont and d'Audrehem charged, therefore, they encountered the archers positioned between the French lines and the prince. These were men of the English vanguard. When the marshals reached the hedge, Salisbury's rearguard rushed forward to assist the archers already engaged in the fight. This also points to the conclusion that the archers were of the vanguard. Additionally, when Warwick saw (or more likely, heard) that the French were attacking while he was yet on the south bank of the Miosson, he 'turned back with his men and crossed the marsh [...] All on horseback, they struck and defeated the shieldbearers'.[188] This last passage from the *Anonimalle Chronicle* confirms the organization of the baggage train's escort. Warwick took with him his mounted men-at-arms, who were ideal for escort duty, and left his dismounted forces, including his longbowmen, posted in their prepared defensive positions. The men that he left on the ridge may have been under the command of the Earl of Oxford, though this is not explicitly stated anywhere.

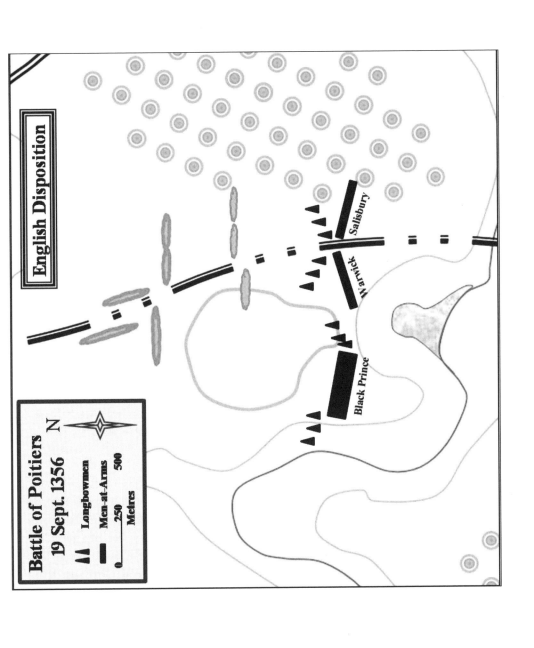

Battle of Poitiers
19 Sept. 1356

▲▲ Longbowmen

■ Men-at-Arms

N

0   250   500
Metres

English Disposition

Salisbury

Warwick

Black Prince

Oxford had been named as a co-commander of the vanguard, and is not anywhere listed among the knights who with Warwick repositioned the baggage trains. Also, later in the battle we will see Oxford personally commanding a contingent of archers, whom he repositions to gain a better angle on their well-armoured French assailants.[189] Thus it would not be unreasonable to conclude that the Earl of Warwick took the mounted contingent of the vanguard with him to lead the baggage trains across the Miosson, and he left the dismounts in the capable hands of the Earl of Oxford.

And how was the Black Prince occupied during this time? When Prince Edward left Nouaillé, he took some of his carts with him to the battlefield, offering further indication that he had no intention of abandoning this hard-won opportunity for battle. Froissart reports that 'on their most exposed side they had placed their carts and other tackle as fortifications, so that they could not be attacked from this quarter'.[190] These would likely have been a few small vehicles carrying the supplies he might need over the course of the battle. The carts themselves would serve another purpose. They anchored the prince's left flank, while his right was tied into the north-west corner of the marshy bowl. Moving along the road heading north towards Poitiers, to which the *Anonimalle* chronicler already alluded, 'the prince's battalion crossed the stream at a fairly narrow ford with their carts and leaving the valley, occupied the hill beyond the marshes and ditches, where they easily concealed their positions among the thickets, lying higher than the enemy'.[191] It was still early in the morning. Warwick's convoy had bottlenecked at the Nouaillé causeway, 'up through the first hour of daylight',[192] and became aware of the French attack a short time later. It was during this period that Edward posted himself atop the hillock west of the marshy bowl. Meanwhile, some of his subordinate knights were occupied in typical pre-battle activities. For an account of these occurrences, Chandos' Herald, concerned above all else with acts of knightly chivalry, is the natural source to turn to.

Prince Edward ordered two knights forward to reconnoitre the French position: 'When it came to early morning the noble and true-hearted Prince called Sir Eustace d'Aubréchicourt with the lion-hearted Lord of Curton, and bade them ride to spy out the French army, and each one set out to ride, mounted on his noble steed.'[193] Froissart's version of events differs primarily on the reason for Eustace's advance, though the two explanations are not necessarily mutually exclusive. Rather than a reconnaissance, the chronicler portrays the advance as an exhibition by 'a young knight most anxious to acquire prowess in arms'.[194] Froissart adds that Sir James Audley, with permission from the Black Prince, 'placed himself in front of all the battalions, accompanied by only four squires from among the most valiant, whom he retained as his personal bodyguard'.[195] Audley then was very likely just to the west of the great hedge, being 'in front of all of the battalions'. He would not have charged from the centre, considering the great number of hedges and ditches that were to the front of the English lines. Another indicator of Audley's line of advance is his target. 'He rode off ahead of the other knights to engage with the battalion of the marshals of France, falling in with Sir Arnoul d'Audrehem and his company.'[196] Marshal d'Audrehem led his troop against the English main body under the prince. Aubrecicourt set out then from the eastern edge, the right flank, of the English position.[197]

This suggestion is also corroborated by what we know of the forces he encountered. If he and the Lord of Curton were advancing from the right flank, they would almost certainly have taken the Maupertuis itself. The terrain on either side of it was too broken to facilitate swift movement. Additionally, Chandos' Herald tells us that d'Aubrecicourt and Curton 'rode so far forward that they were taken and held prisoners'.[198] Advancing along the road they would certainly have had the opportunity to cover a far greater distance than Audley on the left flank in the same amount of time. Also, these two knights met with Jean's foreign knights,[199] who had remained mounted and were accompanying the Constable of France, the Duke of Athens. This troop was advancing south parallel to the west edge of the Nouaillé Wood, along the Maupertuis, and directly towards the English vanguard's position. The advance of the two parties of English knights likely occurred in response to movements by the French marshals, who began their assault, spurred forward against what they believed to be a retreating English army. Froissart tells us that one of the German knights, Ludwig von Recombes, and his men captured d'Aubrecicourt and delivered him to their lord, Count Johann von Nassau, who had the English hostage bound to a baggage cart for the duration of the battle.[200] It is unlikely that he remained tethered to a cart for long, however, because Froissart later tells us that 'as the Germans retreated [during the first phase of the battle] Sir Eustace d'Aubrecicourt was rescued by his men [...] was remounted, and during the rest of the day performed many excellent feats of arms'.[201] It is hardly likely that the German cavalry, who numbered among the constable's shock troops, would have advanced into the mêlée with a cart, which could only serve to impede them. Whatever the conditions of Sir Eustace's brief period of confinement, he clearly did not achieve the same success as Audley had against d'Audrehem's cavalry.

With a reasonable understanding of how the English forces spent the hours before the battle, it is time once again to turn to Jean's army, to observe events in the French camp that fateful morning. Jean, like his adversaries from across the Channel, began the day by celebrating mass. The French had maintained the same position they had taken up two days before, north of the Maupertuis Plain. Never one to miss an opportunity to display his regality, Jean had spent the night in 'a very rich and handsome pavilion of scarlet samite [which he had caused] to be erected on the spot where he had granted the truce'.[202]

Despite the confidence they enjoyed and the apparent ease with which they awaited the battle's start, tensions were mounting in the French army. Many renowned knights were present, and none demonstrated a willingness to allow the English army to escape their clutches. Perhaps the most famous of the rivalries was between the two marshals, Arnoul d'Audrehem and Jean de Clermont. Chandos' Herald records their fiery conversation, which must have occurred only moments before the battle began, just as they witnessed the Black Prince's banner move to the south side of the hill he was occupying:

> The French cried out loudly to the king that the English were fleeing and that they would speedily lose them. Then the French began to ride without longer tarrying. Quoth the Marshal d'Audrehem: 'Certes, little do I esteem your trouble. Soon we shall have lost the English if we set not forth to attack them.' Quoth the Marshal de Clermont: 'Fair brother, you are in sore haste. Do not be so eager, for we shall surely come there betimes, for the English do not flee, but come round at a pace.' Quoth d'Audrehem: 'Your delay will make us lose them at this time.' Then said Clermont: 'By Saint Denis, Marshal, you are very bold.' And then he said to him angrily: 'Indeed you will not be so bold as to acquit yourself today in such wise that you come far enough forward for the point of your lance to reach the rump of my horse.' Thus inflamed with wrath they set out towards the English.[203]

It must be noted here that Marshal Clermont, perhaps the most experienced and competent of the French commanders on the field, was of the clear opinion that the Black Prince was readying to launch an attack, not to escape a battle!

Marshal d'Audrehem, filled with renewed fervour, led his battalion against the men in front of the prince's division, meeting James Audley on the way. Clermont, true to his king's instructions, led the charge against the English archers amongst the hedgerows on the English right flank. Le Baker explains that the conflict between the two marshals had actually begun earlier that morning. Clermont had been one of the foremost advocates of achieving a suitable truce with the Black Prince. The *Chronique des quatre premiers Valois* explains that Clermont counselled King Jean to starve the English into submission, rather than undertaking the 'madness to attack the English where they were'.[204] Marshal d'Audrehem responded that Clermont's advice was the product of fear, not wisdom. His honour thus challenged, and recognizing that battle was inevitable, Clermont received absolution from the cardinal and requested the honour of leading the first charge. His rival, d'Audrehem, however, desired the honour himself, and the two 'argued and strove to leave the other behind'.[205]

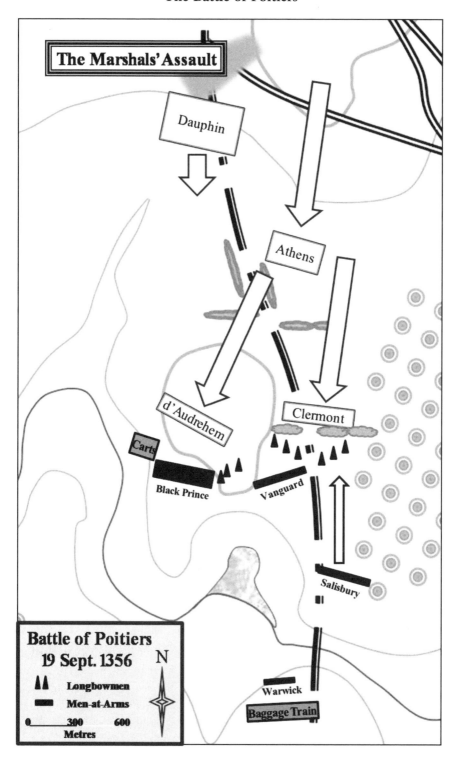

The Marshals' Assault

Dauphin

Athens

d'Audrehem

Clermont

Carts

Black Prince

Vanguard

Salisbury

Battle of Poitiers
19 Sept. 1356
N

▲▲ Longbowmen

▬ Men-at-Arms

0   300   600
Metres

Warwick

Baggage Train

Victory at Poitiers

At the moment the French marshals attacked, the Black Prince and most of the archers were in place, but the Earl of Warwick was still on the south side of the Miosson. We know where Prince Edward had assigned the Earl of Salisbury's division to be, but the chroniclers are silent with regard to his actual location at the time of the first contact. He appears to have been very close to his intended position. Le Baker describes the scene:

> In the upper part of the hedge, well away from the slope, there was a certain open space or gap, made by the carters in autumn, a stone's throw away from which our rearguard was positioned, under the command of the Earl of Salisbury.[206]

The Earl himself was certainly further down the slope. His archers were positioned in and around the hedges forward of his mounted cavalry. Clermont, who led the left column of the French assault, attacked Salisbury's and Warwick's archers at the famous break in the hedge.

The Earl of Salisbury, his cavalry positioned down the south slope of the hill, 'hurried to occupy the gap in the hedge to prevent the enemy from coming through it, and became the first to go into action'.[207] The French attack, meanwhile, had been severely reduced by the well-placed archers. As Clermont rode south along the Maupertuis, the English longbowmen 'began to shoot in quick succession, so effectively from both sides of the lane, sending their barbed arrows deep into the horses' sides that the beasts, smarting under the pain, were too frightened to advance farther'.[208] Clermont, still wishing to overcome d'Audrehem's challenges to his honour,[209] rode directly into the right flank of the English line. John of Fordun at once praises Clermont's fearlessness and denigrates the English tactics, writing that: 'The Marshal of France, with many of the best men of France, thinking to do bravely, burst through the hedges and the vineyards, in hot pursuit of the English; and he there fell, together with all who had come with him, overcome by the archers, and the other ghastly strokes of warcraft.'[210] Many of the mounted French knights had fled when they discovered that they could not break through the English lines, but 'Clermont, who was angry about the words spoken in front of the king, held in place against the English [...] And there the good Marshal de Clermont was killed, for he would not surrender'.[211]

The Anglo-Gascon dismounts did not have to face Clermont's attack alone. Warwick had heard, and probably even seen, the start of the engagement, 'and so the Earl of Warwick turned back with his men and crossed the marsh, finding a good passage which had never before been found'.[212] Historian Richard Barber, author of one of the most celebrated biographies of the Black Prince, agrees that the French marshal's route must have been just to the west of the

Nouaillé Wood, along the Maupertuis, and that Warwick led his counter-attack up that hill from the Gué de l'Homme.[213] His assertion, however, that Warwick was in this position merely by chance, that he was simply recrossing the Miosson 'to report that the causeway at Nouaillé was blocked by carts',[214] is unsubstantiated and in fact makes little tactical sense.

Warwick's men would not have been visible to d'Audrehem had they been at the bottom of the slope, where they recrossed the river between the wood and the marsh, unless d'Audrehem was already at the top of that ridge, at the front line of the English defence. The marshals' orders had been to ride down the archers, spearheading the attack of the closely following dismounted footmen. D'Audrehem, though evidently one of the rasher French commanders, neither abandoned his orders nor rode pell-mell into the fight. Le Baker tells us that he actually 'held back his attack to see what happened' as Clermont's attack developed.[215] He could not have done this if, as Barber indicates, the two marshals were attacking the left and right wings of the English formation separated by the Nouaillé Wood.[216] The two prongs of the French attack were within supporting distance of each other until the last moment when d'Audrehem, seeing the stiff resistance that Clermont was encountering from the English vanguard's archers positioned in the hedges, veered to the west, assaulting the prince's division on the English left flank.

As ill-fated as his charge may appear to have been, Clermont's troop was not completely unsupported in its assault on the English archers. The Duke of Athens, Constable of France, was not far behind the mounted knights. His vanguard, composed of men-at-arms with crossbows and spears, fought against the English men-at-arms: 'then a harsh struggle between the men-at-arms followed, fighting with sword, axes, and lances'.[217] Those that le Baker indicates were fighting with lances were the marshals' select cavalrymen, who had trimmed their lances to 5 feet and removed their spurs so they could better engage the English in close combat on foot.[218] At first Clermont and his men would have attacked from horseback, but the archers killed many of the horses, and the knights would soon be forced to dismount and fight on foot. The English were well-served by their longbows at a distance, but once faced with a close-in mêlée with dismounted men-at arms, they would need a more suitable weapon, and several archers probably discarded their bows for anything they could find, including the lances of fallen French knights.

Meanwhile, Marshal d'Audrehem fared little better against the English left. His troop engaged Sir James Audley and other English knights in front of the prince's position just a few hundred metres to the west. Some sources report that d'Audrehem – in contrast with the stalwart Clermont, whose honour he had just besmirched – fled from the field of battle.[219] Froissart, however, attests that d'Audrehem engaged in personal combat with James Audley, who bested him but did not tarry to claim his prize. Rather, the young English knight continued to fight for the duration of the battle without taking any prisoners for ransom.[220] This display of favouring valour over personal wealth (to be gained by capturing and ransoming enemy knights) stands out as a rarity that day. As we shall see, many Englishmen of all social strata engaged in hostage-taking during the general rout in the later phases of the battle. Audley's actions were not attributable only to his desire to fight, however. The Black Prince had specifically ordered that no prisoners yet be taken, because he wanted to conserve his manpower for the subsequent waves of French attackers. As le Baker notes, 'even though the beginning of the battle had gone well, the hardest work would come when the other battalions came up'.[221]

Certainly, few among the Anglo-Gascon army would have found time to capture or guard even a single Frenchman at this point in the battle. As the constable's men closed with the English rearguard and the dismounts of the van, Warwick crossed back over the Miosson and 'resisted French attackers lower down the slope and in the marsh'.[222] Apparently, some French had managed to run the gauntlet of the hedge-lined road or break through the hedge at the top of the marshy bowl. More likely, they had pushed to the western edge of the hedges lining the Maupertuis and had exploited the gap in the lines between the Black Prince's division and the rest of his army. The Earl of Oxford, who, when the marshals attacked had been at the prince's side (perhaps receiving instructions from the young but capable commander), suddenly identified a weakness in the English defence. The marshals' select, with their horses in barded armour, had been unable to penetrate far into the hedgeline, but the French had found another use for them.

As the French dismounts advanced, the more poorly armoured among them had found themselves vulnerable to the barbed arrows of the English longbowmen. Froissart writes that 'the English archers were an inestimable advantage to their comrades, and struck terror into the hearts of the French, for the rain of arrows was so continuous and so thick that the French did not know where to turn to avoid them, with the result that the English kept gaining ground'.[223] Jean had ordered the marshals' heavily armoured troopers forward because he believed their armour would protect them from the archers. While, due largely to the hedge and ditches, they had failed in their mission of routing the longbowmen, their frontal armour was proving effective against the constant hail of English missiles. The French knights, not without martial talents, innovated a temporary solution that showed promise until an English commander demonstrated that he was able to improvise as well. Le Baker best describes the events that followed:

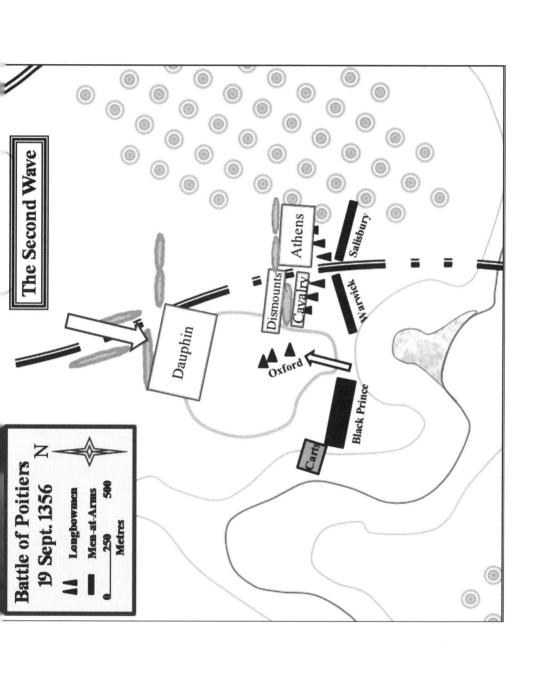

The Second Wave

Battle of Poitiers
19 Sept. 1356

N

▲▲ Longbowmen
▬▬ Men-at-Arms

0   250   500
Metres

Dauphin

Athens

Salisbury

Dismounts

Cavalry

Warwick

Oxford

Black Prince

Carts

The cavalry, designed to ride down the archers and protect their companions from them, stood beside the other French troops and offered the archers as a target only their forequarters, which were well-protected by steel plates and leather shields, so that the arrows aimed at them either shattered, or glanced off heavenwards, falling on friend and foe alike. The Earl of Oxford saw this and left the prince to lead the archers to one side, ordering them to fire at the horses' rearquarters; when this was done the wounded chargers reared, throwing their riders, or turned back on their own men, trampling to death not a few of their masters who had intended quite a different conclusion. Once the warhorses were out of the way, the archers took up their previous position and fired directly at the French flank.[224]

It is difficult to determine with any certainty the exact location of Oxford's manoeuvre, but a survey of the scene suggests that they rushed forward to the security of one of the many hedgelines, from which they could fire on the horses from behind with some degree of safety.

Behind the constable's vanguard another wave of French dismounts were surging forward, under the Dauphin. Le Baker records that they 'advanced without delay'.[225] By this time, Salisbury's still-mounted knights had surged up the slope to the hedge-lined high ground and confronted the French vanguard. With the French assault momentarily halted by Salisbury's counter-attack and the repositioning of the quick-thinking Oxford, Warwick, still mounted, charged up the slope to join Salisbury. There, they confronted the second French division, which was by this point attacking the main line of the hedge.[226] The entire English right had pushed forward to the carters' break in the hedge. The English left, under the Black Prince, moved to close the new gap between the two English wings, advancing forward and to the right. Le Baker states that just before the Dauphin's division reached the English line, 'our men refreshed themselves and the vanguard and centre now merged'.[227] The *Chronique des quatre premiers Valois* confirms that the English by this point had formed a solid line: 'the division of the Duke of Normandy [the Dauphin] neared the division of the prince and both his other divisions, which were united against the Duke of Normandy and the Normans'.[228]

It appears that the Black Prince's advance was something of a counter-attack. Though the chronology of Froissart's account becomes hopelessly jumbled as the battle progresses, he describes events that can be placed in a logical order when paired with information of other more reliable, though often less descriptive, sources. Froissart records that the English main body approached the Dauphin's division in great strength.[229] The *Chronique Valois* for once gives more details than the wordy chronicler: 'And the prince caused his division to advance against the division of the said Duke of Normandy [the Dauphin], and from his division the prince put seven hundred armoured archers behind his men-at-arms, who shot among the faces of the Normans, which did a great deal of damage to them.'[230] The *Anonimalle Chronicle* confirms the occurrence of the prince's action, as well as its results.[231]

Multiple sources pronounce this to be perhaps the hardest portion of the fight. The *Chronique des quatre premiers Valois* calls it 'more amazing, harder and more lethal than the others'.[232] It lasted a long period and filled the air with the sound of battle-cries: 'St George!' by the English, 'St Denis!' by the French, and 'Guyenne!' by the Gascons among them.[233] The fact that the Gascons were among the prince's division helps solidify the claim that the English forces had combined by this point in the battle, since they clearly participated in the defence against the second wave of attack. The only portion of the Anglo-Gascon army that appears to have refrained from joining in the fight to this point is the prince's 400-man mounted reserve. Le Baker tells us that these troops were the only ones under the Black Prince 'who was not either wounded or exhausted by his labours'.[234] The Black Prince had a special role for these knights to play in the battle. King Jean had not yet committed his mounted reserve (or even his third division yet, in fact), and the young prince knew enough to keep fresh his men and their horses. The battle was far from won.

Even so, things were looking bright for Edward's army. The second French division, under the Dauphin, had staggered into this fight, its morale wounded by the sight of the defeated vanguard. Froissart reports that during its advance it 'was closely packed in front, but [...] quickly thinned out behind when they heard that the marshals had been routed, for many of them mounted their horses and rode off ... '[235] The chronicler paints the scene vividly as the Black Prince awaited the third wave of the French assault: 'the marshals' battalion was hopelessly routed, the Duke of Normandy's was breaking up, and most of those who ought to have been fighting were taking to horse and fleeing'.[236] That the king's three eldest sons left the battlefield at this point is uncontested, but the circumstances of their departure are not entirely clear. Le Baker, presenting one of the less flattering accounts, contends that the Dauphin fled the field without even informing his father.[237] The *Anonimalle Chronicle* records merely that the three princes had fled.[238] Similarly, though less specifically, John of Fordun writes that 'the French fled miserably before the face of the English'.[239] The *Chronique Valois*, in contrast – though perhaps as should be expected of the family history – reports that the Dauphin was driven back to his father's position and then ordered into the rearguard, while the king led the final wave. According to this account, only when the king was about to be captured did he order the Dauphin to retire to Normandy.[240]

Froissart seems to agree with le Baker, or at least not contradict his account. The former blames their counsellors for the flight of the young French princes, having them depart along the east road to Chauvigny with 'more than eight hundred lance, fit and sound, who had not been engaged in the battle'.[241] King Jean would miss these knights later. If the princes did flee to Chauvigny as Froissart indicates, it was likely to avoid their father, Jean. Had they ridden north, to the nearer town of Poitiers, to which most of the other stragglers had fled, they would have had to have passed through their father's lines. Even if Jean then ordered them from the field, he most certainly would not have dispatched such a large mounted force with them during the very peak of the battle. When the princes left, the first two French divisions had failed to break the English defence. Jean would not have reduced his number by 800 mailed warriors at such a critical point in the battle. Offering a final explanation, Chandos' Herald gives only a brief explanation of the Dauphin's departure, but this is in character for one who preferred to dwell on acts of valour. He writes simply that: 'The division of Normandy was discomfited that morning, and the Dauphin departed thence.'[242] This source, at least, confirms the amount of time that had elapsed to this point in the battle. It was not yet noon, but there was still more fighting to come.

As the Dauphin and his brothers fell back, their uncle, the Duke of Orléans, advanced. Little is written about the actions of his division. In fact, as we have seen, some historians doubt whether his battalion ever engaged the English at all. The *Anonimalle Chronicle* suggests that Orléans' division fared little better than had his nephew's.[243] Much in the same way as the rear of the Dauphin's division had 'thinned out' before it had even advanced, as it retreated from the field it would have passed by, and sometimes through, the French third division, and a number of Orléans' men almost certainly joined in the flight. Froissart goes so far as to say that the men of the third division, 'complete and unhurt [...] had left the field and were then in the rear of the king's own battalion'.[244] The chronicler here offers a scenario that could likely explain the jumbled flight and subsequent reorganization of the French divisions. The French princes, seemingly of their own volition, though likely on the advice of panicked advisors, fled the Maupertuis Plain by a route that would not expose them to the condemning gaze of their father the king or of his attending knights. No source lists them among either the casualties or the captured. Additionally, a large contingent of mounted soldiers left the field with them. Most of the French soldiers, however, remained in the fight. Those who could, rallied on King Jean. Froissart writes that 'there were many good knights and squires who, though their commanders had left the field, refused to retreat, preferring to die rather than to be reproached with having fled'.[245] The *Anonimalle Chronicle* numbers those who flocked to the king's banner at '8,000 bascinets, along with a great number of shield-bearers, crossbowmen, and other infantry'.[246] Le Baker echoes the claim with less specificity.[247] Chandos' Herald writes that Jean assembled 'a great power, for to him drew every man who would fain acquit himself well […] it was a marvel to behold'.[248]

Thus far it would appear that the English had acquitted themselves with all honour and that the French had performed poorly at best. The prince's men were not without their fault, however. Despite the issue of strict guidance that no prisoners were to be taken until the battle had completely run its course, at least one of the Black Prince's knights found himself caught up in the excitement of the rout, to his own detriment. Geoffrey le Baker relates the following tale:

> Our men, however, realising that the honours of the field were still dubious as long as the usurper and his forces might still be hidden in some nearby valley, did not leave their place to pursue the fugitives. But that hero worthy of his illustrious line, Sir Maurice Berkeley, son of Sir Thomas, thought otherwise […] He plunged into the Dauphin's division and laid about him with his sword, not thinking of flight so long as a Frenchman remained standing in his sight. He never looked back to see where his men were, nor looked at the standards in the air, but pursued the Dauphin's soldiers alone. Having broken his lance, sword and other weapons on them by the strength of his blows, he was overpowered by force of numbers, and taken for ransom, horribly wounded and unconscious.[249]

Clearly Berkeley was operating outside the bounds of prudence, and apparently without having been ordered forward on a perilous mission, such as Sir Eustace's failed reconnaissance. Berkeley, however, may not have been the maverick that he at first appears. He was not alone in pursuing the fleeing French, and he may have been acting as part of a larger, more legitimate force.

After the rout of Orléans' division, the French appeared to be in full flight. Against this third wave, which, due to its collision with the second, was disorganized almost beyond recognition, the defenders under the Black Prince expended their energy as well as their ammunition. Henry Knighton reports that 'the English were exhausted by the intensity of the battle, and their weapons were much worn. And so strong and so hard was the fight that the archers ran out of arrows, and picked up stones, and fought with swords and lances, and anything that they could find, and they defended themselves with marvellous courage, and at last as God willed it the French took to flight.'[250] As the French soldiers fled, many of them back to the city walls of Poitiers, a good part of the mounted Anglo-Gascons saw their opportunity to complete the victory by engaging in the most one-sided phase of any battle: the pursuit. The Earl of

Warwick seems to have been at the head of a troop of horsemen who chased the fleeing French for some distance. Various sources describe the Earl's pursuit as taking place during different phases of the battle, but it most likely occurred during the lull after the repulse of the Duke of Orléans' division.

The outnumbered Englishmen desired reprieve and the lull that followed must have encouraged some that the battle at this point might have reached its end. But the Anglo-Gascon army's exhaustion was apparent to the French as well, and Jean was not yet defeated. William Douglas, the highly esteemed Scot, at this point advised King Jean that he could still secure a victory, despite the tactical defeat that must have seemed as inevitable as it was shocking.[251] The conditions that had brought the Black Prince to battle had not changed. He was still in enemy territory and outnumbered, and the English still had nothing to eat or feed to their horses. Both sides were exhausted from the morning's combat, but whereas the French king could expect a continuous flow of reinforcements, there would be no succour for the English. If Jean withdrew even to the plains between him and the walls of Poitiers, he could establish a defensive position that the Black Prince would be foolish to attack. Thus, having to choose between assuming the tactical offence and starving to death, Edward would be forced to offer terms. Jean probably spent many months contemplating the wisdom of this advice from the confines of the Tower of London, but he did not choose to accept it now. Instead, Jean 'swore an inviolable oath that he would not abandon the battlefield that day unless taken or killed and removed by force'.[252]

Jean rather advanced his banners and ordered all of his men to dismount, which he himself did. Even the remnant of his army far outnumbered the English men-at-arms, and he knew that it would not take much to break the fragile morale of his enemy's spent force. The French king's numbers had swollen from a 400-man reserve to a unit of several thousand. The size of his force at this point led some chroniclers to label it a fourth division. Froissart indicates that many men of Orléans' division were still fresh even now.[253] They had evidently avoided the slaughter that so many others of the second and third division had been caught in, particularly during the prince's advance or flanking manoeuvre. The English army was now, however, spread right across the field and beyond. Jean noted this and it further emboldened the French soldiers. The king advanced 'with a huge force, directing his attack towards the prince, who had few men with him at that moment, because the rest were pursuing the defeated enemy'.[254] Jean must have been an imposing figure, wielding his battleaxe and surrounded by thousands of armoured men-at-arms.[255] Delacroix immortalized the scene in his painting, *John the Good and his son at Poitiers*.

The Battle of Poitiers

The Black Prince was undaunted, despite the fact that the English had suffered from hard fighting and now faced King Jean leading the largest division of the day. While many of the attackers were fresh, the Anglo-Gascons were far from rested. Many of the defenders had fallen casualty during the first three assaults, the archers had all but exhausted their store of arrows, and the Earl of Warwick had left the field with a large body of the most fit men, in pursuit of the fleeing French of the previous divisions. While both English and French sources comment on the French deserters, no one mentions any Englishmen abandoning their prince. This may not be a mere nod to the victors that day; it is quite possibly true that very few, if any, English soldiers fled that day. They would have realized they had little hope of reaching sanctuary travelling alone through hostile countryside, and they did not have enough supplies on hand to provide for themselves even if they did attempt to run.

Those that had left the field were not fleeing but pursuing, and Warwick was at their head. Berkeley's chase may have been part of this greater action, or it may have been its inspiration, but on this point we have no documentary evidence. What we do know is that le Baker did not criticize the young knight's action, even though it resulted in his capture. Thus it may not have been as anomalous as his accusers would first have us believe. Additionally, we can infer that Berkeley made his foray during or after the retreat of the second and third French lines, but before the king assembled his fourth division. Not only does le Baker's account support this chronology, but if Berkeley had been captured any later, he certainly would not have been held for ransom. He most likely was captured by a knight or group of knights that shuttled him back to the safety of Poitiers before the defeat of Jean's division. Similarly, we do not know exactly when Warwick began his pursuit or how far it carried him from the prince, but Henry Knighton tells us at what moment he returned: 'just as the French line bore down, the Earl of Warwick returned from the chase with his whole force, and took the French army in the flank'.[256] The *Anonimalle Chronicle* does not specifically state that Warwick had ever engaged in the premature pursuit, but does tell us that he and twenty bascinets and twelve archers joined the Black Prince just as Jean attacked.[257]

This final phase of the battle stands apart from the rest by its very nature. The French king, with several thousand dismounted men-at-arms and archers, advanced his banner and marched to meet the Black Prince in the middle of a large open field between their positions. The English soldiers may have expected to repeat their proven tactic of defending from prepared positions, but they knew that this was not to be. The archers would not be able to contribute in the same manner as they had to this point with such effect. Almost without arrows, they could hardly be expected to fire as before, when they had been 'an

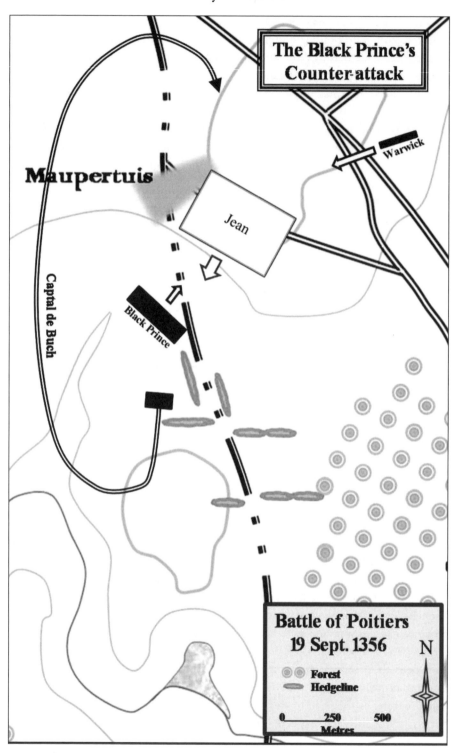

The Black Prince's
Counter-attack

Warwick

Maupertuis

Jean

Captal de Buch

Black Prince

Battle of Poitiers
19 Sept. 1356

N

Forest
Hedgeline

0   250   500
Metres

inestimable advantage to their comrades, and struck terror into the hearts of the French, for the rain of arrows was so continuous and so thick that the French did not know where to turn to avoid them'.[258] Since many of the mounted men-at-arms were absent from the field, running the Dauphin's men to ground, the prince's men were right to feel forlorn. But the Black Prince rebuked the suggestion that victory was not still within their grasp, though those with him 'were frightened not only by the numbers of the enemy but also by their own considerably weakened state'.[259]

But this was the fight he was waiting for. He had demonstrated his capabilities as a tactical commander. Now he wished to demonstrate his prowess in individual combat. That he could not retreat and therefore had no other option but to advance should not detract from the fact that he made the decision to attack rather than surrender. A less confident commander may have given up at this point. He welcomed the danger to his person, and coveted the glory that he knew would result from it, win or lose. The chroniclers were also aware of the valour demonstrated by the decision of the two commanders. In each case the name of their respective banner bearer is recorded, such was the honour bestowed upon the man advancing the colours. Le Baker tells us that it was Sir Walter Woodland[260] who received the order from the prince, though it is from Froissart that we know the words: 'Ride on, bannerer, in the name of God and Saint George!'[261] Similarly, Jean's colours were carried by Sir Geoffroi de Chargny, but he, like all other Frenchmen participating in the advance, moved forward on foot.[262] From their orders we see that the final clash was of the French reserve against a mounted English counter-attack. Edward had completely abandoned the defence, the security of the ditches, hedges, vineyards and slopes, and threw everything he had remaining into one final, desperate assault.

As the Black Prince urged his men forward, one of his Gascon subordinates, the Captal de Buch, recognized a tactical opportunity. He suggested that he lead a force of sixty knights and 100 archers, all mounted, in a flanking manoeuvre to the French division's rear.[263] The prince and his army were outnumbered and no longer had the benefit of the defence to compensate for their numerical disadvantage. The Captal de Buch's tactic might help level the playing field. The prince wisely assented, and the troop rode off, breaking from the main body and heading south. In order for the manoeuvre to work, they had to descend from the view of the French only reappearing to their rear. This meant that they also had to disappear from the view of their English and Gascon brethren, the vast majority of whom would not have been privy to the plan. Instead, those ignorant of the Captal de Buch's mission assumed that they were fleeing the field.[264] The French likely interpreted the troop's departure in much the same way, and would have been encouraged by the sight. The Black Prince, probably more confident with his secret knowledge of the bold tactic, rode forward, his charge announced by a wild din of blaring trumpets.[265] Le Baker, in a rare display of flowery prose, recounts the scene in vivid detail:

> With a handful of men [the Black Prince] met the usurper's army. The trumpets sounded and clarions, warhorns and drums replied, until the sounds echoed along the Poitevin Woods, until the hills seemed to roar to the valleys and the clouds of thunder. Nor did these thunders lack thunderbolts, for the light sparkled golden on the armour, and the flying arrows cascaded from polished shields, their points finding their mark like thunderbolts.[266]

As the prince's division attacked the French front, Warwick bore down on the enemy's left flank.[267] He had returned from his pursuit, perhaps alerted to the battle's climax by the horns and drums. What may seem to have been an ill-timed departure from the field now aided the English cause, as it provided for an attack from multiple angles. It must also be remembered that Warwick, mounted, was driving into the side of an entirely dismounted French formation. The shock of his horsemen would have been devastating to the trudging infantrymen, particularly since his attack struck them at an unexpected angle. The few arrows that the prince's archers had left proved to have little effect. The French soldiers easily shielded themselves from any missiles directed against their fronts, and longbows were once again discarded for any available weapon that could be found among the dead and dying. The hundred archers among the Captal de Buch's troop, however, managed much greater results. They, mounted and striking against the French rear, found much easier targets for their arrows.

The exact route of the flanking manoeuvre is unclear and hotly debated. Many historians – from Sir Charles Oman, writing at the end of the nineteenth century, to those as recent as Jonathan Sumption, writing at the turn of the millennium – have contended that the Captal de Buch's force rode round the extreme left flank of the French, striking Jean's division from the north-east.[268] This interpretation is predicated upon the placement of the English line (and hence most of the fighting) north, rather than west of the Nouaillé Wood. Hewitt takes the unique position correctly identifying the battlefield west of the wood, straddling the Maupertuis, but then when describing the Captal de Buch's ride, follows the convention of the easterly route. This option seems to have been accepted wholesale without sufficient consideration.

The battlefield was west of the wood, on the plain just north of the Miosson, on a site now largely (and most unfortunately) occupied by a small housing development. The modern presence of the hedgeline along this ridge is certainly insufficient to draw any solid conclusions, but the intransigence of such terrain features does contribute to the likelihood of the claim's accuracy. Noted historian, Jim Bradbury, when he writes that 'since we cannot place the site precisely, can we allow considerations about a site which some historians believe to be correct to influence an interpretation of tactics. In other words, we must rely only on the contemporary evidence',[269] goes too far in countering Burne's practice of solving historical enigmas by applying modern tactical theory.[270] To use a metaphor from mathematics, history is a series of multi-variable equations; solving for one unknown assists us in determining the values of the rest. The fact that if we err in our initial calculations the accuracy of the entire equation suffers should inspire us to proceed with our calculations as scrupulously as possible, not discourage us from attempting to formulate an answer at all.

One of the key points of the chroniclers' descriptions of the battlefield is the low hill from which the Black Prince commanded the battle. Not only is there nothing resembling a hill to the north of the Nouaillé Wood, but even if there were, no one crossing the Miosson at either the causeway in Nouaillé or the ford at the Gué de l'Homme, or at any other point along its course, would be able to see the French attack as the author of the *Anonimalle Chronicle* claims he did in the previously cited passage. The continuation of this account provides valuable clues to the battlefield's location and must be reconsidered here.

> And the Earl of Warwick crossed a narrow causeway over a marsh where he found a French town with a castle […] And then they saw the vanguard of the French come towards the prince with two large divisions of men-at-arms, shield-bearers, and crossbowmen. And so the Earl of Warwick turned back with his men and crossed the marsh, finding a good passage which had never before been found.[271]

The Earl's ford is today spanned by a small bridge, located between the wood and the marshy bowl. Had Warwick somehow been able to see the prince getting attacked at a position north of the wood (the conventional location is 2 kilometres due north of the Nouaillé bridge, through the forest) he certainly would not have ventured to the west of the wood – a route that would have increased the distance he had to ride by at least 50 per cent, especially since, according to the sources, he did not know whether there was any site at which he could cross the river west of the town. No, he would have ridden back as directly as possible, even if he were trying to flank the French vanguard.

In addition to the conventional location of the battle lacking a hilltop, it also lacks a marsh. Le Baker clearly describes a hill beyond 'a broad deep valley and marsh, watered by a stream'.[272] He can only be referring to the hill north-west of the marshy bowl, as there is nothing resembling a marsh to the north of the

Nouaillé Wood. There is certainly not a long slope leading down to a marsh, such as le Baker describes Warwick's vanguard defending.

If, therefore, we accept the location to the west of the woods alongside the Maupertuis as the correct location for the battlefield, we must reassess the likely route that the Captal de Buch could have taken to encircle King Jean's division. Le Baker again provides the most detailed description:

> The Captal de Buch made a wide sweep, retreating down the slope of the hill which he and the prince had recently left and circling the battlefield, reached a point below the original position of the usurper [Jean]. From there he rode up to the battlefield by the path just taken by the French and suddenly burst out of hiding.[273]

The prevalence of hedges at the time makes almost any point in the area a possible location from which he could 'burst out of hiding', but the other clues are more helpful. As the Captal de Buch descended 'the hill which he and the prince had recently left', he would first have to have returned to it, since the prince had since advanced the entire line forward to meet the preceding attacks. He therefore would be approaching the hill from the north. It would make little sense for him to descend the hill again along its northern slope, because that would just return him to the prince's position. If he circled to the east, he would have to skirt the northern edge of the marshy bowl, cross behind the entire defensive line, and then either through the Nouaillé Wood, and around it to the north. Although there is and probably was an east–west road bisecting the wood that he could have taken, it seems unlikely he would have chosen this course. If he had, as he rounded the northern edge of the wood, he undoubtedly would have become entangled in the fleeing masses, and perhaps even met up with Warwick's troop on their return. Neither of these events is mentioned or even suggested in any source. If he had ridden down the southern slope of the hill he would have to have crossed the Miosson, found his way through unexplored territory to the west, and recrossed the river at a new, previously unidentified ford site. This also is unlikely. The final and most plausible alternative is that he descended the west slope of the hill, perhaps behind the cover afforded by the prince's obstacle of carts, and followed the woodline to the north. He may even have entered the wood for additional concealment. This route would allow him to 'circle the battlefield' while still maintaining his bearing relative to the battle. He could then re-emerge to the north of the ridge, behind which Jean had originally arrayed his divisions, and ride uphill to the battlefield upon which the French were advancing on foot against the single division under the Black Prince. This is the route the Captal de Buch followed as he crested the ridge and waved the banner of St George, signalling to the prince that he was prepared to attack.[274]

In one final note on this point, it must be considered that Burne, Sumption and other noted historians depict de Buch's troop as heading easterly, or even north-easterly.[275] Le Baker, however, notes that the English soldiers, the vast majority of which would not have been privy to the new plan, 'thought they were fleeing. Our army, except for the leaders, despaired of victory because of this, and commended themselves to God.'[276] If the mounted force was truly heading in the direction that these earlier historians suggest, the troops would have been heading deeper into enemy territory, not towards the sanctuary that fleeing troops would have sought. The onlooking soldiers would more likely have believed that the Captal de Buch's men were following Warwick, who had departed the field in the same direction. Also, one must remember that the Captal de Buch had plenty of time to ride in any direction he chose. He and his men were mounted, while the French king was leading a dismounted assault over several hundred metres of broken terrain. The Captal de Buch led his men off the field heading south towards Gascony, where he was from. He disappeared from view and that is why the soldiers despaired. He had taken the same route the watching soldiers would have taken if they themselves were Gascons fleeing the field.

But the Gascons did not flee. They circled the French army's position, advancing along the same route their enemies had just traversed, and struck them in the rear. At approximately the same time Warwick returned from his pursuit of the second and third French divisions and attacked the French flank. The Black Prince had mounted his horse and led a charge against the French front. The French dismounts would have parried the frontal assault easily – they had a tremendous numerical advantage and, as already discussed, the English longbowmen could accomplish little against their well-armoured fronts, especially with the paucity of arrows remaining. With the limited resistance to their front and the strikes against their left flank and rear, the French surged forward, driving back the prince's division. Since many of the English soldiers would not have been mounted by this point, some advanced piecemeal against the attacking French. These were 'the other English and Gascons [who] rallied to him from all over the field'.[277] The Black Prince, for his part, was not to be outdone by any knight that day, friend or foe:

> He rushed through the confusion of the battle line, sending those he met in hand-to-hand fighting vanquished to the underworld, and hastened threateningly towards the usurper's bodyguard, still in closely [*sic*] order behind their solid shields. Then banners and their bearers began to fall; here men trampled on their own guts, others spat out their teeth; many were hewn to the ground, lost limbs while still standing. Dying men rolled in the blood of others, groaned under the weight of the fallen, and with

proud hearts, groaned as they left their unworthy bodies. The blood of slaves and princes ran down in one stream to empurple the nearby river and frighten the fish with this delicate nectar.[278]

The honour of striking down the French king's standards did not go to the prince, however. The Captal de Buch had this singular honour, though he did not manage to capture the king.[279]

Jean, by all accounts, fought as well as any man on the field at Poitiers. He made good his promise not to leave the fight by his own power. Froissart calls him fearless and 'a good knight and a lusty fighter'.[280] Jean de Venette, a prominent Carmelite friar who was a contemporary of the battle though not a witness to it, serves to inform us on the Parisian perspective on their king's valour. For Venette, King Jean's capture is a tragedy, but not one that he brought upon himself:

> King John came to battle in high spirits. He desired to fight on foot with his men, and this he did. After he had sent away his horses, he entered the conflict and attacked the enemy boldly and bravely. He slew several and wounded many mortally. Had all the nobles and knights borne themselves as bravely as the king they would have triumphed gloriously over all their enemies. But many, become pusillanimous and sluggish, were loath to attack their adversaries. The English, emboldened by this, made a spirited attack on King John. Though he defended himself manfully and slew many, he could not withstand so overwhelming an attack.[281]

As he fought, the mêlée drifted south, passing over the hill on which the prince had begun his defensive stand, and continuing down the hill to the Miosson. There, at a point known as the Champ d'Alexandre, the French king, despite his valour, began to succumb to the English onslaught. Le Baker writes that Jean, 'although full of years, showed the zeal of a young knight, doing great deeds, training some, killing others, cutting or bruising faces, gutting or beheading others. He showed by everything he did that he was no unworthy descendent of French kings.'[282] Jean was hardly 'full of years', even compared to the Black Prince. The king was 37 to the prince's 26. Even so, accompanied by his youngest son, Philip, Jean battled the English attacks until the small group of loyal knights around him could defend him no more. He fought even after he had sustained an injury to his face, having been cut by the stroke of a sword.[283] In the end he surrendered. The question of to whom he surrendered, however, is no clearer than any other aspect of the battle. Nor was the matter easily resolved in the days following.

As should be expected by this point in our study of the events at Poitiers, the sources disagree on the number of casualties and some of the details of the battle's outcome. Some chronicles, such as those of John of Fordun, the *Anonimalle* and the *Chronique Valois*, do not attribute Jean's capture to any particular individual. Perhaps for a Scot or a Frenchman the key fact was that their kingdom's greatest champion had been captured, and the name of the captor was simply inconsequential. To the writers of the English perspective, however, this detail mattered a great deal. Le Baker credits the Black Prince himself, writing that 'the prince of Wales charged into the enemy with the wild courage of a lion; he tamed the pride, spared the fallen and accepted the surrender of the usurper'.[284] Chandos' Herald is more specious in his language, but certainly gives at least indirect credit to Prince Edward: 'the prince made such onslaught that [the king of France] was taken by force … '[285] The prince, in his dispatch to the Londoners, did not take credit himself, but left the question of the name of the captor open.[286] Froissart, as might be guessed, provides a rather detailed account of the king's capture. And the honour does not go to the prince. According to Froissart, when Jean found that his situation had become hopeless, and that the greatest knights in his retinue had already been captured or killed, he looked about the battlefield for the Black Prince so that he could surrender to him. The Black Prince was not in the immediate vicinity, but Sir Denis de Morbecque, a French knight from Artois who had been previously exiled for murder,

> was fortunate enough to be nearest of all those around the king of France when his capture became imminent; he accordingly jostled his way through the throng by means of his great strength, and said to the king in good French, to which the king listened more readily than to that of the others, 'My lord, my lord, surrender yourself.'[287]

Jean had at first preferred to surrender to a fellow royal. Failing this, he surrendered to an estranged Frenchman on the prince's behalf.

Apparently others crowded around Jean, the battle's ultimate prize, each protesting their own right to his capture, and, implicitly, his ransom.[288] The argument continued, becoming more heated until the Earl of Warwick arrived on the scene. As the battle progressed it had become more and more chaotic. Some Frenchmen had broken ranks and fled, following the example of the Dauphin and Orléans. The soldiers of the Anglo-Gascon army naturally pursued them. They could sense that the time had come to turn their focus to the acquisition of personal wealth. Victory, once de Buch had struck down the French king's standards, was assured: 'Realising that the standard of the lilies had fallen, they fled as fast as they could to the nearby city. The English, although either badly wounded or extremely weary, out of joy at having saved their lives and won the day, pursued the French up to the gates.'[289] An unusually high number of captives were taken that day, but the Black Prince had one particular hostage that he wanted in his possession above all others. Ignorant of the fate of his adversary the king, Prince Edward raised his banner at the top of a small hill to signal the return of his victorious army. He then sent the Earl of Warwick and the Lord of Cobham to find him the king. It was at this point that they stumbled upon the argument over his capture already in progress. The two nobles took possession of King Jean and brought him to the prince.[290] The king of France would eventually be brought back to London and presented to his rival, the Black Prince's father, Edward III. Several other of the most prominent captives changed hands as well. Those who had accepted their surrenders were, of course, compensated.

Jean, as has been noted, was but one of many knights captured that day. Many knights had been killed over the course of the battle, including the constable and Marshal Clermont, as well as Geoffroi de Charny and Eustace de Ribemont. Henry Knighton gives a comprehensive record of those captured and killed. Besides Jean and his son Philip, he lists eleven counts and an archbishop.[291] Medieval sources, as we have seen, often present inflated or otherwise inaccurate counts of soldiers, whether at the beginning of a battle or in the counts of dead and wounded. Knighton reports that the French suffered 2,300 killed and 2,500 captured over the course of the battle.[292] The *Anonimalle Chronicle* numbers the captured French at ninety-two banners.[293] Froissart's tallies are much higher. He states that the French suffered 5,700–6,000 dead, the vast majority of which must have been unknighted combatants.[294] With only 3,000 knights in the French army to begin with, at least half of the dead must have been the other soldiers, and since the English soldiers would have been more likely to take knights captive before they would other combatants, a far greater portion of the dead would have been from the lower ranks. Bartholomew Burghersh, present at the battle, states that thirty-one distinguished prisoners, as well as 'a further 2,500 persons, of whom 2,000 were men-at-arms', were taken by the prince's men.[295] Similarly, he reports '2,800 killed, including 2,000 men-at-arms'.[296] John Capgrave reports 2,000 captured and more than 5,000 dead.[297]

While Froissart does not give an exact number for those captured, he writes that there were twice as many hostages as there were captors.[298] If he was referring to the entire Anglo-Gascon army, this would constitute an improbably large number of captives. He had earlier reported that the English fielded 'no more than eight thousand men', so allowing for meagre English casualties, this would suggest approximately 15,000 captives, or about one-third of the total French force by his estimation.[299] If, instead, we assume that Froissart was referring to the English men-at-arms only, whom he had numbered at 2,000, the tally of captives would correspondingly reduce to 4,000, or even fewer, if we concede that a good part of the English men-at-arms were at this point still pursuing fleeing Frenchmen. Chandos' Herald reports more moderate numbers of perhaps 1,100 captured and 3,000 dead.[300]

However many men were taken prisoner that day, it was far more than the Black Prince wanted to have in tow as he marched to Bordeaux. Though he had the French king in his possession, the Dauphin and two of his brothers had escaped, and the force that the French princes had taken with them from the battle surely outnumbered the beleaguered Anglo-Gascon army. Even if it did not, men loyal to Jean would likely have rallied to the Dauphin had he attempted to rescue his father, and the prince's army was already slowed by the tremendous stores of booty it had gathered on the *chevauchée* earlier in the campaign. The Dauphin probably should have attacked or at least pursued the Black Prince at this point.[301] He knew that the Anglo-Gascon army was already dangerously short of provisions even before the battle, and the Black Prince could not have long refused a seat at the bargaining table had the Dauphin blocked his route to Bordeaux. Recognizing this truth perhaps more than did his adversary, the Black Prince strove to move as quickly as possible to the safety of his Gascon holdings. Many of the captives, therefore, were released on the spot, usually after they had pledged to pay their ransom by Christmas.[302] Neither le Baker nor John of Fordun provide estimates for the numbers of casualties. The *Chronique des quatre premiers Valois* lists the most notable captives taken, and supports the conclusion that most of the dead were non-noble, by adding that 'an amazing number of men, as well as dukes, counts, barons, knights, esquires and good footmen (*servans*) were killed'.[303] Thus there were some nobles killed, but the majority of the deaths were of mere *men*.

No recent historian has ventured to precisely number those killed that day on the Maupertuis plain. Lieutenant Colonel Alfred H. Burne, writing in 1955, used inventive processes of conjecture to answer many otherwise indeterminable details of this and other campaigns. He is so confident of his estimate on this point that he uses it as a basis for his one of his four parallel calculations of the total size of the French army at the start of the battle:

> Approximately 2,500 French are reported killed, and 2,000 captured. If we allow two men wounded for one killed that would make the total casualties including captured about 8,500. In so heavy a defeat as this one might expect the casualties to amount to nearly 50 per cent of combatants, which would thus be 17,000. To this we must add the 5,000 or so of Orleans' division which presumably had no casualties. This brings the grand total to approximately 23,000.[304]

More credible historians, such as Sumption and Rogers, each accept the figure of 2,500 noble men-at-arms dead, but refrain from extrapolating the total number killed, which was surely much greater.[305] Hewitt acknowledges a suggested figure of 'about 2,000 men-at-arms and 800 others' that he draws from a conglomeration of sources, but endorses neither it nor the only two estimates of deaths of English nobles at the battle: forty and sixty, which he suggests 'may be dismissed as valueless'.[306] Froissart and Knighton each provide extensive lists of the French dead[307] but neither acknowledges significant English casualties. Hewitt briefly contends that the nature of the combat must have resulted in high English casualties,[308] but neither offers any evidence of this, nor attempts to determine an estimate.

A final detail of the battle that has proven somewhat contentious is the issue of precisely when it began and how long it lasted. Most accounts of the battle do not report a specific time, as the medieval conception of time was not married to the hands of the clock, as it is now. A few clues do exist, however, which can help us establish a likely start time and duration for the actions on 19 September. Chandos' Herald states that Sir Eustace d'Aubrecicourt began his short-lived reconnaissance 'when it came to early morning'.[309] According to this account, once news of this action spread it spurred the prince's repositioning to the reverse slope of the hill on which he was situated, which effectively drove the French marshals to action. This description fits with that provided by Froissart, who alone provides specific times for the battle: 'It commenced about nine o'clock, and was ended by noon; but the English were not all returned from the pursuit [...] They did not return till late after vespers [4 p.m.] from pursuing the enemy.'[310]

Most modern historians seem to accept this timeline for the battle, though Burne offers a different position. Noting that the weekend truce had ended at 7.30 on Monday morning, he 'cannot accept Froissart's unsupported statement that the battle began at "prime" and ended at "nones": more likely it began at "nones" (noon) and ended at vespers (4 p.m.)'.[311] Sumption, too, makes a curious assessment, stating that the battle 'lasted longer than any other major engagement of the period, with the result that they ran out of arrows long before the end'.[312] The battle proper – that is everything until the final rout, at which point Jean and Philippe were captured and the general rout began – did not last longer than four hours by anyone's count. Sumption does not appear to be including the final wild pursuit of the fleeing French as part of the battle, because by then the English archers had long since cast away their missile-less longbows and 'left their positions and fell on the French with knives and swords, followed by the men-at-arms'.[313] In any case, the battle of Crécy had lasted an extraordinary seven hours – twice as long as Poitiers.

The Battle of Poitiers

When the Black Prince had signalled the end of the battle by planting his standard atop a hill, the English soldiers, some who had chased the French as far as the walls of Poitiers,[314] slowly made their way back to their victorious commander, nearly all of them with captives in tow. Le Baker reports that trumpets sounded a call for the far-flung English soldiers to return, and this would certainly have been more effective than merely raising the prince's banner.[315] Froissart tells us that the English established a camp in the immediate vicinity of the battlefield, and that they at once began to tend to their prisoners.[316] Le Baker adds that they cared for the wounded – French and English alike – and sent out search parties for their missing comrades.[317]

The most famous of those unaccounted for, and the one for whom the prince was most eager for news, was Sir James Audley. Some of the prince's knights found Audley 'among those half dead and scarcely breathing',[318] and bore him on either a litter or a large shield to the pavilion that the Black Prince had had erected and which was now serving as his command post.[319] The pavilion itself may have been part of the spoils of war. It could have been the same magnificent scarlet tentage in which Jean had spent the last days and hours before the battle.[320] The victors were eating the food of the vanquished, so why not sleep in their tents as well? Froissart suggests that the prince spoke with Audley before Jean was brought to his pavilion, whereas le Baker reports the opposite order of events, even having the Black Prince excuse himself from dinner with the captured king to go visit Audley once news of his condition finally arrived.[321] The two chroniclers agree, however, on the perception of Audley's conduct during the battle. The prince was so grateful to his friend that in a characteristic act of generosity, he granted him an annual pension of 500 marks (we know that in 1346 a man-at-arms was paid 1s per day, and this rate likely would have changed little by the time of the Poitiers campaign. Thus, at 20 shillings to the pound, the pension the Black Prince granted Audley was sufficient to hire a company of over 100 men-at-arms for a period of two months). In the conversation reported by Froissart, Audley demonstrated that his chivalrousness matched his lord's:

> When he was come into his presence, the prince bent down over him and embraced him, saying: 'My lord James, I am bound to honour you very much, for by your valour this day, you have acquired glory and renown above us all, and your prowess has proved you the bravest knight.' Lord James replied: 'My lord, you have a right to say whatever you please, but I wish it were as you have said. If I have this day been forward to serve you, it has been to accomplish a vow that I had made, and it ought not to be thought so much of.' 'Sir James,' answered the prince, 'I and all the rest

deem you the bravest knight on our side in this battle, and to increase your renown, and furnish you withal to pursue your career of glory in war, I retain you henceforward, for ever, as my knight, with five hundred marks of yearly revenue, which I will secure to you from my estates in England.'[322]

Audley, ever the model of humility and generosity, had his bearers return him to his own tent, and then called in his brother and four other knights, including Bartholomew Burghersh (who makes no mention of the episode in his brief account of the battle) as witnesses to the fact that he surrendered the prince's gift of revenue in its entirety to his four squires.[323]

The prince, by all accounts, was a gracious host to King Jean, treating him with great respect and even personally serving him wine and dinner.[324] Froissart records the Black Prince's address to his royal captive:

Dear sir, do not make a poor meal because the Almighty One has not gratified your wishes in the event of this day; for be assured that my lord and father will show you every honour and friendship in his power, and will arrange your ransom so reasonably, that you will henceforth always remain friends. In my opinion, you have cause to be glad that the success of this battle did not turn out as you desired; for you have this day acquired such high renown for prowess, that you have surpassed all the best knights on your side. I do not, dear sir, say this to flatter you, for all those of our side who have seen and observed the actions of each party, have unanimously allowed this to be your due, and decree you prize and garland for it.[325]

The prince's words may have comforted Jean a little on some level. As previously noted, his reputation had suffered much while his subjects waited for him to defend his realm from the English *chevauchée*. It can hardly be suggested, however, that his increase in personal glory was any consolation for the uncertainty that now faced him over the future of his kingdom. His marshals killed or captured, his army dispersed, Lancaster's army rampant in Normandy, and now both he and King David of Scotland in Edward's hands, English victory must have seemed all but certain. And not all of the dangers were foreign. Charles of Navarre had been conspiring against Jean while the French king was yet free. Now that he was captive, he had reason for concern that the crown would no longer be his once liberated. Edward III had laid claim to the French crown nearly twenty years before. Now, at the very least, he would press his demands for full suzerainty in Aquitaine and perhaps even the old Angevin holdings in Normandy, Anjou and Maine. Calais was still firmly in English hands. Even if Jean managed to keep his crown upon release (and he must have noted that David had been in captivity for ten years thus far), France might be a much-reduced and poorer kingdom than it had been only months before.

Tuesday, 20 September

In the morning the English army began its journey south to Bordeaux, undoubtedly anxious to distance itself, heavy-laden as it was, from the Dauphin and the remains of the French army. In all, the Black Prince at the head of his small Anglo-Gascon army had accomplished more in six weeks than any other campaign of any duration had (or would) throughout the entirety of the war. Raids are notoriously expensive affairs when one considers the cost of raising, equipping, transporting and feeding an army. The 1356 *chevauchée*, culminating with the battle of Poitiers, not only ended with all of the key French commanders captured or dead (besides the king, Marshal d'Audrehem was prisoner, and Marshal Clermont and the Constable, the Duke of Athens, were dead, leaving only the 18-year-old Dauphin at large), but so many other notable hostages had been taken that their ransom is estimated to have paid for the entire year's campaigning three times over.[326] How, then, was Edward III to capitalize on his son's success?

Aftermath

———— •)(•) ————

N

ow that the Black Prince had had his battle and emerged the undisputed victor, there was no question that he should return to Bordeaux. What other options existed? Should he have pursued the fleeing Dauphin? Poitiers was a strong city, and the French that had escaped death or capture on the Maupertuis plain still outnumbered the English and Gascon soldiers, who were, it must be remembered, critically short on supplies even before the battle began. Any lingering would leave the Black Prince's men vulnerable to counterattack. He would not risk losing possession of his most valuable prize: King Jean. Froissart remarks on the immense satisfaction the prince and his men felt as they made their way south: 'They were so laden with gold, silver, jewels, and great prisoners, that they did not attack any fortress in their march, but thought they should do great things if they were able to convey the king of France and his son, with all their booty, in safety to the city of Bordeaux.'[327]

As soon as the heralds had performed their key role of identifying the dead, and once the question of ownership of prisoners had for the most part been settled, the march began. The pace was steady and deliberate. The greater part of the army was in Bordeaux by 2 October. In twelve days they covered nearly 150 miles, never pausing for long at any city along the way. The directness of the route is further evidence of the Black Prince's intentions for the campaign. When he found that there would be no pursuit, he could have ordered his men to advance to the south, ravaging a wide swath through French territory that had thus far escaped the English sword. But the prince's *chevauchées* had one purpose: to bring the French army to battle. Now he had done that, and he had won.

In medieval writing weather often serves as an indicator of God's pleasure with the course of human events. Chandos' Herald must have considered the Almighty very pleased with the Black Prince's success, because by his account, He graced the English with fair weather for their return to England, their precious cargo in tow. Once there, the celebrating began in earnest.

[As] soon as they had landed, they sent to the king the news that were good and fair to him. He ordered all his barons to meet him, as a mark of honour. He came in his own person, and with him more than twenty earls; they escorted the prince, whom they greeted, to London. There were they well entertained by the ladies and so welcomed, that never, so the true God glad my heart, was there such rejoicing shown, as was made at this time. There was the noble powerful king, with the queen, his wife, and his mother, whom he held right dear; they caused many a dame and damsel, very lovely, frisky and fair, to dance and hunt and hawk, and make great festivities and jousts, as in the reign of Arthur for the space of four years or more.[328]

The rejoicing in London was matched by anger and panic in Paris. Their king was captive! Froissart records that the nobles who had escaped Jean's fate at Poitiers returned to the French capital at their own peril. The townspeople blamed them for their humiliation.[329] The French were not helpless without their king, however. Representatives of the three estates met, directed the collection of taxes, negotiated for Jean's release, and did what they could to prevent lawlessness from overtaking the countryside. It was not mere bandits who roamed through France now, as had been the case in the years leading up to the momentous battle. English garrisons throughout the kingdom took advantage of the weakness of the Dauphin to seize additional lands. These activities were not restricted to nobles, either. The *Scalachronica* records that:

> Many fine deeds of arms befell the English in this time in diverse places in the realm of France [...] These Englishmen, on their own accounts, had set themselves up in many places in the realm of France during this war – common people, young, unknowns from various regions of England, many of them starting as archers and then becoming knights, some even captains.[330]

The outlook was bleaker for France now than it had been ten years before. The horrific defeat at Crécy might have been considered a fluke, but after Poitiers who could but question the course the war was taking? Crécy had been only a short distance from the Channel; Poitiers had been fought in the very heart of France. Many had died at Crécy but more had fled from Poitiers. Which was the greater shame? One had not fled – Jean. The king had fought to the end of his powers, but now he was in the hands of the English and France was in the hands of deserters.

Though Jean was prisoner, one should not imagine him in chains, dirty and miserable. Multiple sources indicate that the prince treated him with every respect in the days following the battle. He was given as spacious accommodations as possible during the twelve-day voyage from Bordeaux to England, and, though under stiff guard, he was always treated with dignity. His treatment stemmed not only from his royal blood. Jean had proven himself a worthy knight on the fields of Poitiers, and he was, besides, first cousin of Edward III's mother, Isabella of France. He never need fear for his life. If nothing else, he could rest easy with the knowledge that he remained valuable to the English only so long as he was alive. Assured though it may have been, his release was not as easily achieved as either he or Edward would have preferred.

The Treaty of Brétigny

'We Charles, governour of Frauns, the first begotin son of John, Kyng of Frauns, upon the Holy Sacrament swere here, and on the Holy Gospelle, that we shal kepe pees and concord which is mad betwix the Kyngis, and make no contradiccion ageyn it.'[331] Thus the Dauphin swore to uphold the terms of the Treaty of Brétigny, which, after over three years of captivity, secured King Jean's release. The period between the Poitiers disaster and the resolution of the peace was among the most horrific in medieval France. The oft-quoted chronicle of Jean de Venette describes in vivid detail the conditions of life for the common people:

> The English destroyed, burned, and plundered many little towns and villages in this part of the diocese of Beauvais, capturing or even killing the inhabitants […] No wayfarers went along the roads, carrying their best cheese and dairy produce to market. Throughout the parishes and villages, alas! went forth no mendicants to hear confessions and to preach in Lent but rather robbers and thieves to carry off openly whatever they could find. Houses and churches no longer presented a smiling appearance with newly repaired roofs but rather the lamentable spectacle of scattered, smoking ruins to which they had been reduced by devouring flames […] The pleasant sound of bells was heard indeed, not as a summons to divine worship, but as a warning of hostile incursions … [332]

It was a period of civil war. Historian H.J. Hewitt writes that:

> In large measure, the king was the state: it was the king personally that the royal officers served; it was to the king personally that the lords were bound by homage […] Sectional leaders arose, discredited counsellors came forward, the evil genius of Charles of Navarre was ever close at hand. But of strong leaders capable of putting the national interest before all others, there were none.[333]

Victory at Poitiers

Interestingly, a positive aspect of the Treaty of Brétigny – one that perhaps made possible France's ultimate victory in the Hundred Years War – is the centralization of French state power that arose from the depths of the post-Poitiers chaos. This chaos must of course be understood before its reversal can be appreciated. The greatest contributor to French lawlessness after Poitiers was, undoubtedly, the foreign captivity of the French king.

Such was the situation in France, with no one exercising central authority, that the struggle between Lancaster, as Edward's lieutenant in Normandy, and various constituent cities continued into the summer of 1357. Edward pledged to order Lancaster to halt his siege of Rennes, but all of the king's instructions did not reach his commander until after the operation's conclusion.[334] Nonetheless, a two-year truce was formally in effect beginning in the spring of 1357. The French must have been glad for the respite from wholesale invasion, but the widespread marauding by uncontrollable *routiers* and Free Companies and by partisans of Charles of Navarre continued, further eroding the Dauphin's power. Edward, meanwhile, felt so confident of his advantage that he finally released King David of Scotland after eleven years' captivity in the Tower of London with the signing of the Treaty of Berwick on 3 October 1357.[335]

The negotiations continued into the autumn and winter of 1357; thus, the first formal draft for a settled peace was not to come until more than a year had passed after the battle. These terms were in January 1358 presented to the Dauphin, who seems to have been appreciative of their leniency.[336] The proposal stipulated that Jean would relinquish all claim to an expanded Duchy of Aquitaine and that he would pay a hefty ransom. When Edward's Parliament met in February to consider the treaty, the assembly must have felt very confident of the powerful diplomatic position that England enjoyed, and decided to use the situation to press the resolution of unrelated conflicts with the pope, a known supporter of Jean.[337] Another attempt was made at ratification in the summer of 1358, resulting in the First Treaty of London. This treaty had four key components. First, it granted Edward full sovereignty over all the lands that Richard I had held in Aquitaine, plus those in the region controlled at the time of the Black Prince's victory at Poitiers. Second, it secured for Edward and his successors Calais and its environs in perpetuity. Third, it demanded a ransom of 4 million gold *écus* (over twenty times the annual revenue of the English crown for the year 1300) and stipulated a payment plan, a clause that acknowledged the tremendous magnitude of the sum. Finally, the treaty required that Jean and all his subordinate parties forever abandon any collusion with the Scots.[338]

With Jean in the Tower of London and both Normandy and Gascony not only subdued but occupied, Edward appeared to have unprecedented leverage in his negotiations over the issues that had spawned the war in 1337. The chief points of contention, it must be remembered, were the possession of the French

Aftermath

throne, the sovereignty of Aquitaine, and French interference in English affairs with Scotland. Each of these, it would seem, could, by Christmas 1356, easily have been resolved in Edward's favour; but resolutions were not as simply achieved as one would expect. The nobles in both Scotland and France were slow to amass the requisite ransoms, not least because the kingdoms' regents were in no rush to relinquish their new-found powers back to the kings who, by their captures, had so ineptly burdened their kingdoms. They had each, in effect, truly become 'a national liability'.[339] Honour would not allow their subjects, relatives and countrymen to abandon them, but the economic and, more importantly, the political cost of gaining their return might prove ruinous. David's ransom had been set at 100,000 marks (£66,666). The amount Edward demanded for Jean was ten times that – a sum that the teenage Dauphin had not the bureaucratic systems in place to raise. It was the territorial demands that the English king put forth, however, that the French found less palatable.

The French having failed to meet the demands of the First Treaty of London, Edward prepared yet another invasion force and drafted a second, much more severe treaty dated 24 June 1359. In addition to all of the demands of the previous treaty, it called for the surrender of Touraine, Anjou, Normandy and the County of Boulogne – in effect, a generous reconstitution of the Angevin empire.[340] In the meantime, however, not all had progressed in Edward's favour. The civil war in France had worn down his greatest Continental ally, Charles of Navarre, who had surprised everyone by reconciling himself with the Dauphin.[341] With new-found optimism the French regent and his council rejected the Second Treaty of London, because, in the words of le Bel, 'the said peace seemed to be too damaging for the realm of France in several ways, and they would rather continue to endure the misery in which they found themselves, and which King Jean suffered, and await the pleasure of God, than to consent that the noble realm should be thus lessened and divided by the said peace'.[342] It is often overlooked, however, that the second treaty did soften on one point: Jean's ransom was effectively reduced by one quarter.[343]

Edward's 1359–1360 campaign has received considerable criticism as a failure at both the tactical and strategic levels of war. It is true that he did not accomplish his apparent purpose of capturing not only Paris, but Rheims, the traditional French coronation site; yet the campaign did ultimately lead to the signing of the Treaty of Brétigny. The English army divided into three components for the ensuing campaign, described in the *Anonimalle Chronicle*. The Duke of Lancaster led the initial invasion, leaving from Calais and conducting a devastating *chevauchée* along the Flemish border, and circling back along the Somme. The Black Prince led a second division, along with his brother, the Earl of Richmond, as well as the Earls of Stafford and Northampton. Edward himself led the third division, accompanied by the well-known Earls of

Warwick, Suffolk, Salisbury and Oxford. The three commanders spent the remainder of the year ravaging the countryside around Rheims, never more than a few days march from each other, causing great unrest in the territory previously not subject to the English raids.[344] The *Scalachronica* details the next two months, during which time they conducted innumerable independent operations, seizing many towns and castles. By the end of February Burgundy had made peace with Edward to avoid further devastation.[345]

By 8 April 1360 Edward was before the walls of Paris. Within, the Dauphin and his brothers and uncle – all of whom had fled Poitiers – had no desire to face the English king in combat. Instead, they began to treat for peace. Meanwhile, Edward continued his raids, but had little hope of taking either Paris or Rheims. It is impossible to know for sure whether the proud Plantagenet had ever had designs on besieging the great cities. He had clear memories of the year he spent outside the walls of Calais and probably hoped that the cities would request surrender terms fairly quickly. One historian suggests that Edward's situation was more precarious than his French enemies probably realized, writing that 'Edward's purpose was to force a treaty on the government of the Dauphin while he still had an army in the field and while there were still supplies in the region to feed it. Terrorism on a great scale was Edward's only means of doing this.'[346] However, the French certainly understood the limitations of Edward's army. The resulting Treaty of Brétigny did not require the surrender of the old Angevin lands of Normandy, Touraine, Maine and Anjou. It very closely resembled the First Treaty of London, with the addition of a clause by which Edward would renounce any claim to the throne of France in exchange for Jean's cession of full sovereignty for an expanded Aquitaine, which was implicit in the first treaty.[347] While some modern commentators have been tempted to paint the campaign as an expensive failure, since the resulting treaty was less favourable for the English than had been the treaty proposed before Edward set sail, this would be a short-sighted interpretation. The goal of the campaign was to bring the French to the bargaining table – an event they had been avoiding for over three years. This Edward accomplished. That the treaty did not end the war – or did not permanently do so – is the product of entirely separate issues.

The terms proposed by the Treaty of Brétigny were finally ratified by the two monarchs six months later as the Treaty of Calais. The key difference between the two treaties was that, perhaps the most important clause – the renunciation of rights that each king was to make – were moved to a separate document, conditional upon the fulfilment of certain other requirements, such as the transfer of lands and castles. With the new treaty signed and a down payment made on Jean's ransom, the French king was finally released. The key stipulations, however, were never met, the renunciations never made. The chance for lasting peace at France's expense thus eluded the English king and his

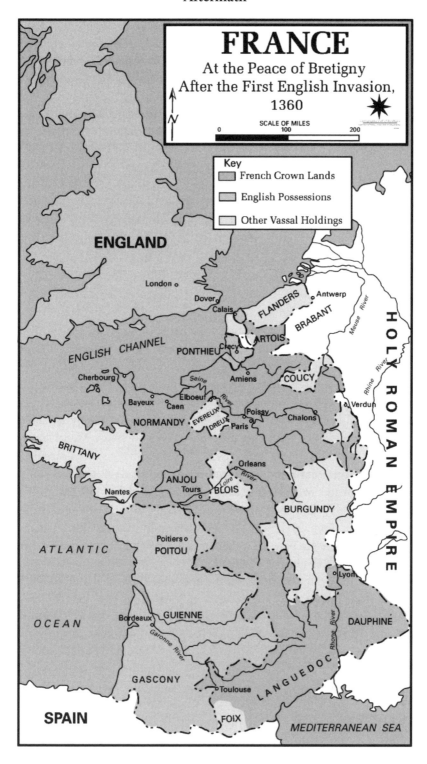

FRANCE

At the Peace of Bretigny
After the First English Invasion,
1360

SCALE OF MILES
0   100   200

Key
French Crown Lands
English Possessions
Other Vassal Holdings

ENGLAND

London
Dover
Calais
FLANDERS
Antwerp
BRABANT
ARTOIS
Crecy
PONTHIEU
ENGLISH CHANNEL
Meuse River
Rhine River
HOLY ROMAN EMPIRE
Cherbourg
Seine
Amiens
COUCY
Bayeux
Elboeuf
Caen
Poissy
Verdun
NORMANDY
EVEREUX
DREUX
Paris
Chalons
BRITTANY
Orleans
Nantes
ANJOU
Tours
BLOIS
Loire River
BURGUNDY
Poitiers
POITOU
ATLANTIC
Lyon
Bordeaux
GUIENNE
Garonne River
DAUPHINE
OCEAN
Rhone River
GASCONY
Toulouse
LANGUEDOC
SPAIN
FOIX
MEDITERRANEAN SEA

ambassadors. In a typical interpretation of national strengths, the Treaty of Calais has sometimes been portrayed as ultimately representing more of a French victory: 'Edward, that is to say, who had harvested his military victories at Brétigny, was defeated by French subtlety at Calais.'[348]

A weil commendit man, off wertu, manheide and bownte[349]

'A well-commended man, of virtue, manhood and bounty.' The Black Prince had, by all accounts, done much to earn this description. Certainly, he had been given every advantage. At age 3 he was Earl of Chester, by 7, the first to hold the title of 'duke' in English history, and by 13, the Prince of Wales. Even more instrumental to his development than the titles bestowed upon him was the tutelage and mentorship he received. His father was perhaps the most lauded commander of his age, and the men of the king's retinue, including Grosmont, Salisbury, Warwick and the Captal de Buch, were often of equal ability (or very nearly so). It is not a common thing in English history for a father and son to both be of martial renown, but in Edward III and the Black Prince we find a true example of this occurrence. Empty titles aside, by 16 the Black Prince had demonstrated his courage and tenacity at the battle of Crécy and throughout the campaign that had led up to it. Eight years later he commanded a famously daring and profitable raid through Languedoc, and not long after his twenty-fifth birthday he found himself on the Maupertuis plain, amid fields strewn with his fallen enemy, and himself in possession of his father's fiercest rival.

The story of Edward of Woodstock, known most commonly as 'the Black Prince' to later ages, does not end at Poitiers. Even so, many would lament his life as all too short. Five years later, in 1361, after receiving special dispensation, he broke with the long-standing tradition [of tremendous political utility] of taking a Continental wife. He married his cousin, a childhood friend, Joan of Kent. They spent several years at court in Gascony, in the fashion of his great-great-great-uncle, Richard 'Lionheart', who had spent most of his reign abroad. Their son, the future Richard II, rather than the Black Prince, would eventually succeed Edward III as king of England.

His time in Bordeaux and its environs undoubtedly contributed to the Black Prince's interest in Spanish politics. In 1367, the same year that Richard was born, the prince sided with the exiled Pedro of Castile (also known as Pedro the Cruel) at the battle of Najera. This battle bore many resemblances to those with which both sides would have been familiar: Crécy, Neville's Cross and Poitiers, among others. One should not be surprised to find it so. Some prominent heroes of those earlier battles were present at Najera, including the Captal de Buch and John Chandos. There were new faces, too, however, including the Black Prince's younger brother, known as John of Gaunt. The Franco-Spanish contingent was over-reliant on its cavalry. The English-led invasion force pushed deep into enemy territory, and then dismounted and assumed the tactical defence, trusting in flanks of longbowmen to repulse the assaults against the infantry centres, and once again 'arrows flew thicker than rain in wintertime'.[350] The Black Prince had won yet another hard-fought contest against his father's enemies.

The battle between the Black Prince and Bertrand du Guesclin holds double importance, and both facets contribute greatly to French domination in the next phase of the Hundred Years War, though one would be hard-pressed to argue which was the dominant factor. It is widely held that it was during the prince's Spanish campaigns that he contracted the disease to which he would fall victim in 1375, after having returned to England. Edward of Woodstock would never become Edward IV. He would leave that name to a later Edward. At the age of 45, one year before his father's own death, the Black Prince died. The Prince's death not only deprived England of a great and proven commander, but the coronation of his 8-year-old son, Richard II, opened the door to domestic disputes, and, ultimately, regime change at the hands of John of Gaunt.

The second key result of the campaign between the Black Prince and du Guesclin was the strategic vision that the latter gained from suffering yet another tactical defeat at the hands of the English. Du Guesclin formulated a strategy that must have been difficult for knights of the chivalric age to adopt. He embraced the Fabian practice of avoiding battle – trading space for time. Employing what would become common practice in the later Age of Limited Warfare (nominally 1648–1792), the objects of his campaigns would not be the glorious decisive battles that the Edwards always sought, but rather the more deliberate and methodical practice of avoidance of battle in favour of the reduction and subsequent occupation of strongpoints. This type of campaign would characterize the next phase of the Hundred Years War, in which French successes would compensate for the losses incurred during the years of Edward III's reign.

It may additionally be argued that the Spanish campaign contributed a third cause for the improved French showing in the second phase of the war. Edward's support of Pedro the Cruel alienated the supporters of the eventual King of Castile, Pedro's brother, Henry of Trastamara. Castilian ships played a large role in supplanting English domination of the Channel, limiting trade, blocking invasion, and ever threatening French amphibious assaults. The Black Prince's incursions south of the Pyrenees certainly cannot be blamed entirely for the English misfortunes of the last decades of the fourteenth century, but neither can their role be dismissed.

The nature of the negotiations for the Treaty of Brétigny proved to be, unfortunately for the English, symptomatic of the last two-thirds of the Hundred Years War. There would continue to be great displays of valour. Heroes such as Henry of Grosmont, Lord John Talbot and King Henry V would emerge. But in the end, England found itself out-strategized by France. In truth, the Continental power had, as has been noted, most of the matériel advantages throughout the entire war, but its leaders had for too long failed to capitalize on its natural strengths.

One commander who grasped the type of war that France should be fighting was Bertrand du Guesclin. Despite being roughly the same age as the Black Prince, and each in his military prime during a period of persistent conflict between the two kingdoms, the two commanders met surprisingly few times. The battle of Najera, briefly discussed earlier, is perhaps the most famous of their contests. There, the prince was victorious and du Guesclin was captured. The French commander from Brittany did not favour large-scale battles, but preferred smaller engagements with more focused objectives. As a result some historians have labelled him a guerrilla. This title may be accurate, but one should focus on du Guesclin's adeptness at identifying appropriate targets of opportunity and his inventiveness in attaining victory, rather than romanticizing his role as a leader of the French resistance. He was conventionally trained, mentored by Marshal Arnoul d'Audrehem of Poitiers fame. Regardless of his methods, he was one of the most highly respected commanders of the entire war, and any of the kings involved would probably have relished the opportunity to employ him in their camp. Had his loyalty lay with his regional Breton lords rather than with the French king, the war might have ended very differently. Like the Black Prince, du Guesclin died at an early age from an illness contracted while on campaign. At the age of 40 he fell victim to dysentery, but not before he had reversed the victories that the English had achieved between 1346 and 1360.

Battles could provide dazzling results, and many commanders in the Age of Chivalry sought them for their potential decisiveness, but even the most glorious victories, such as those at Crécy and Poitiers, produced little, if any, lasting effect. Nor did the *Grande Chevauchée* of 1355 of itself permanently alter the course of the war in France. Du Guesclin had understood that the war was to be won through the control of population centres. It may be fair to reach the conclusion that English commanders did not, for the most part, share this wider strategic view, or that if they did, they did not consider it to be practical (with their very limited resources) to man the numerous garrisons that would be required to hold the land once conquered. One commander exemplifying the English predilection for swift actions directed at enemy military forces was Henry of Grosmont. He was of Edward III's generation, rather than a contemporary of the Black Prince, du Guesclin and John Chandos. His name appears on the rolls of some of the most famous engagements of the era, including Sluys, the siege of Calais, Aiguillon, the Rheims campaign of 1359–1360, and (perhaps) even Halidon Hill in his earlier days. He was absent from Crécy and Poitiers only

Aftermath

because Edward trusted him with independent commands. During the Crécy campaign, Henry of Grosmont, later Duke of Lancaster, commanded the southern army of the three-pronged invasion. At every opportunity he sought to advance England's strategic situation through feats of arms. He conducted his operations masterfully, but none were able to translate their momentary success to permanent victory. He shared the vision of the two Edwards, but perhaps too closely. It would take a new king with a new strategic outlook to turn around the effort to preserve England's rapidly disintegrating Continental holdings.

Edward III died in 1377, one year after his eldest son and namesake. The Black Prince's son, Richard II, succeeded him, and it is surprising that he sat on the throne for as long as he did. The twenty-two years of his reign are remembered for the rampant civil unrest, especially during the Peasants' Revolt of 1381, the Lords Appellant's rebellion of 1387, and the king's deposition in 1399. It may be claimed that his reign had been doomed from the start, since he was only 10 when he ascended the throne, but one must remember that Edward III was not much older when he was crowned under far more scandalous circumstances. Henry of Bolingbroke was the eldest son of John of Gaunt, the Black Prince's younger brother. John had been a peacemaker between the two cousins, Henry and Richard, and when John died in 1399, Henry raised an army of malcontents against Richard, had him imprisoned, and assumed the throne. Crowned Henry IV, he reigned until 1413.

Though the French were in the midst of their own domestic power struggles, Charles VI took advantage of his rival's inability to enact any sort of military counter to his incursions into Gascony. Less than ten years into Henry's reign, little was left of the lands acquired by his grandfather, Edward III. When Henry V assumed the throne upon his father's death, he faced a desperate situation on the Continent, or so it seemed. Civil strife was ebbing in England just as it was peaking in France. The Burgundians and Armagnacs were endeavouring to seize power in Paris. Henry V decided to act. His 1415 invasion, from the siege of Harfleur to his implausible victory at Agincourt, has become, literally, the subject of legend. English kings during this period all suffered from the same inability to follow tremendous battlefield victories with equally decisive treaties. Henry V came closest, with the Treaty of Troyes in 1420, which saw him named heir to the French throne and Regent of France, but he died only two years later before he could reap the benefit of this singular diplomatic victory. The coronation of his 8-month-old son, Henry VI, did little to further English political objectives.

The Duke of Bedford, Henry V's brother, was serving as regent when he had his remarkable victory over the French and allied forces, including a contingent of Scots – who died to the last man – at Verneuil in 1424. But the time when a decisive battle could win the war for the English had passed. Even though Henry VI was crowned king of France in Paris in 1431, within five years Charles VII

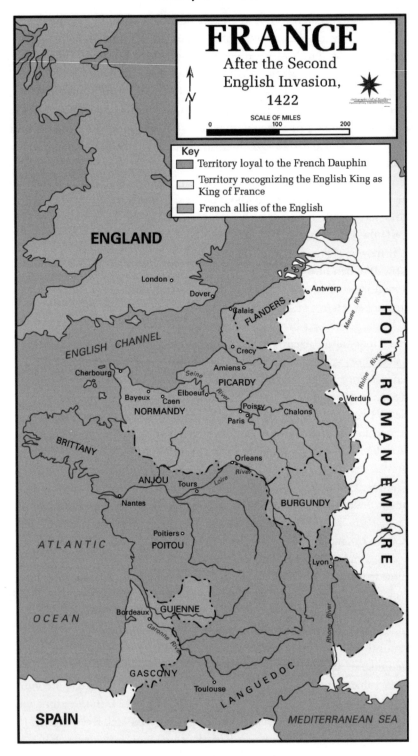

FRANCE

After the Second
English Invasion,
1422

SCALE OF MILES

0   100   200

Key

Territory loyal to the French Dauphin

Territory recognizing the English King as
King of France

French allies of the English

ENGLAND

London

Dover

Antwerp

Calais

FLANDERS

Crecy

ENGLISH CHANNEL

Amiens

Cherbourg

Seine

PICARDY

Bayeux Elboeuf

Caen

NORMANDY

Poissy

Chalons

Paris

Verdun

BRITTANY

Orleans

Loire River

ANJOU Tours

Nantes

BURGUNDY

ATLANTIC

Poitiers

POITOU

Lyon

OCEAN

Bordeaux GUIENNE

Garonne River

GASCONY

Toulouse

LANGUEDOC

Rhone River

HOLY ROMAN EMPIRE

Meuse River

Rhine River

SPAIN

MEDITERRANEAN SEA

Aftermath

had recaptured the capital city, and the tide had forever turned. By 1451, the old Angevin empire, including Normandy and Maine, had fallen into French hands, and even Gascony had been wrested from English control.

Charles VII, however, was unpopular with leading Gascons, who had been under Plantagenet control for 300 years. They invited an English invasion, which Lord John Talbot led in 1452. The ensuing uprising reclaimed most Gascon cities for England, beginning with Bordeaux, but when Talbot rushed to pursue the French he believed to be retreating from the siege of Castillon the following year, he, his son, and nearly every man in their army fell in a hail of French artillery fire. This would be the last battle of the Hundred Years War. It was one of the most disastrous tactical missteps an English commander had made during the war, but it signifies the advent of the centralization of the French state. The French king, having resolved the domestic infighting that had plagued the kingdom for generations, was marshalling his resources and financing the development of perhaps the most revolutionary military technology in the history of the world. At the same time, there was no doubt that there would be no Plantagenet counter-offensive to reclaim Gascony. It was England's turn for civil war: the Wars of the Roses.

Notes and Sources

1. Sir Charles W.C. Oman, *The Art of War in the Middle Ages* (Ithaca, New York: Cornell University Press, 1885), 116.
2. Oliver J. Thatcher and Edgar Holmes McNeal, eds, *A Source Book for Medieval History* (New York: Scribner's, 1905), 412.
3. Clifford J. Rogers, 'Edward III and the Dialectics of Strategy, 1327–1360' in *The Wars of Edward III, Sources and Interpretations*, ed. Clifford Rogers (Woodbridge, Vermont: Boydell Press, 1999), 265–84.
4. Oman, *The Art of War*, 122.
5. The treaty provided that: 'the land taken from the king of France in the Duchy […] should be restored without delay […] and similarly the lands which the king of France, or his people, have occupied in the Duchy […] should without delay be restored to the king of England.' The indemnity of 50,000 marks was to be payable on demand, held to assure Edward's cooperation. 'The Treaty of Paris, March 1327', in *English Historical Documents IV 1327–1485*, ed. David C. Douglas (New York: Oxford University Press, 1969), 49.
6. For a more in-depth discussion of the 'feudal' and 'dynastic' schools, read Anne Curry, *The Hundred Years War* 2nd Edition (New York: Palgrave Macmillan, 1993, 2003), 28–50.
7. The subject of negotiations between the two kings will be discussed later in the section on the Treaty of Brétigny.
8. Richard Barber, *Edward, Prince of Wales and Aquitaine* (New York: Scribner's, 1978), 33.
9. For a thorough account of Edward's situation and operations in 1337–1340, see Clifford Rogers, *War Cruel and Sharp* (Rochester, New York: Boydell Press, 2000), 157–216.
10. Froissart (Johnes) v1, 57.
11. Fowler, *Hundred Years War* (London: Macmillan, 1971), 17.
12. For a detailed account of Sluys, see Jonathan Sumption's, *The Hundred Years War Vol. I: Trial by Battle* (Philadelphia: University of Pennsylvania, 1991), 319–29.
13. The three ancient battles of Trebia, Lake Trasimene and Cannae do not bear great tactical resemblance to Crécy, Poitiers and Agincourt, but each won great fame for its victor, though the seeming decisiveness of each proved short-lived.

14. For the best examination of the battle of Morlaix, see Kelly DeVries, *Infantry Warfare in the Early Fourteenth Century* (Rochester, New York: Boydell Press, 1996), 137–44.

15. Froissart (Johnes) v1, 117–25.

16. Rogers, *Sources*, 107. Froissart repeats this assessment in Chapter CVI, when the count assembled Gascon forces to besiege Auberoche later that year (1345), and 'they all obeyed his summons; for he was as a king in those parts of Gascony'. (*Sources*, 113.)

17. Barber, *Campaigns of the Black Prince*, 14.

18. Barber, *Campaigns of the Black Prince*, 27.

19. *The Hundred Years War*, trans. Peter E. Thompson, 59.

20. *Chroniques*, Stock, 1997, 109.

21. Rogers, *Sources*, 123.

22. Chandos Herald, *Le Prince Noir*, eds Mildred K. Pope and Eleanor C. Lodge (New York: AMC Press, 1979), lines 115–21; Sir Thomas Gray, *The Scalachronica: The Reigns of Edward I, Edward II and Edward III*, trans. Sir Herbert Maxwell (Felinfach, Wales: Llanerch, 2000), 114.

23. Rogers, *Sources*, 123. Henry of Knighton indicates that the French fleet had begun to assemble, however, because Edward 'found there thirty great ships and galleys, which he took'. Henry Knighton, *Knighton's Chronicle 1337–1396* (New York: Oxford University Press, 1995). A letter from Michael Northburgh, dated 27 July 1346 reports that Edward's troops captured and burned a total of twenty 'ships with castles fore and aft' at the ports of la Hogue and Barfleur, in addition to many smaller boats. They burnt an additional sixty-one warships 'along the sea coast from Roche Masse to Ouistreham'. (Barber, 15–17.)

24. Jean le Bel, *Contemporary Chronicles of the Hundred Years War: from the works of Jean le Bel, Jean Froissart & Enguerrand de Monstrelet*, ed. and trans. Peter E. Thompson (London Folio Society, 1966), 60.

25. Le Bel, 61.

26. Knighton, 55.

27. Chandos' Herald, lines 169–70.

28. Northburgh, Barber, 15.

29. Andrew Ayton, 'The Crécy Campaign', in *The Battle of Crécy, 1346* (Rochester, New York: Boydell Press, 2005), 62–72.

30. Chandos' Herald reports that Edward, before disembarking his ship onto the Cotentin, 'knighted the prince, the Earl of March also, and the Earl of Salisbury, John of Montagu, his brother, and others, more than I could tell you'. (Lines 145–53.) The *Acts of War* has the ceremony taking place 'on a high hill near the shore' and adds William le Ros, Roger de la Warre and Richard de la Vere to the companions (Barber, 27). Bartholomew Burghersh and the Chancellor of St Paul's, who were both eyewitnesses, make similar reports.

31. Chandos' Herald (lines 2603–18).

Notes and Sources

32. Froissart (Johnes) v1, 152.

33. Letter of Edward III from Caen, Rogers, *Sources*, 124.

34. Barber, *Acts of War*, 38–9.

35. This sentiment is echoed in *The Chronicle of Henry Knighton*, where the author discusses the French plan to repeat William's 1066 conquest of England. But Edward's 1346 campaign pre-empted Philip's attack: 'God struck them with such terror by our king's blessed advent in those parts that they abandoned the whole plan, and so on that occasion their scheme was undone.' (59.) For the best examination of events at Blanchetaque, read Andrew Ayton's 'The Crécy Campaign', in *The Battle of Crécy, 1346*, Andrew Ayton and Sir Philip Preston (Rochester, New York: Boydell Press, 2005), 85–100.

36. John Capgrave, *Capgrave's Chronicle of England* (London: Longman, Brown, Green, Longmans, and Roberts, 1858), 211–12.

37. Froissart, 160.

38. Froissart, 161.

39. Froissart, 160.

40. Clifford Rogers discusses two other possible identities of the informant, and argues that Edward may likely have discovered the ford even without the assistance (*War Cruel and Sharp*, 262–3, 263n). Philip in any case had apparently expected Edward to find it, because he detailed a large force to defend the north bank.

41. Knighton, 61.

42. Chandos' Herald, lines 261–3.

43. 'King Edward's Own Account, from Caen through Calais', *Wars of Edward III*, 130.

44. Knighton, 61.

45. Froissart, 161.

46. From the eyewitness account of Robert Northburgh. (*War Cruel and Sharp*, 262–3n.) Ayton also accepts this estimate ('The Crécy Campaign', 96).

47. Capgrave reports 2,000 Frenchmen killed (212). Knighton writes that the English 'killed 2,000 men-at-arms and more of the commons' (61). Neither Froissart nor Chandos' Herald give estimates, but each remark that many French fled.

48. Froissart, 161–2. Edward III confirms Froissart's story, writing that 'quite soon after we had crossed the river, our said adversary [Philip] showed up on the other side with a great force of men so suddenly that we had no warning at all'. ('King Edward's Own Account', 128.)

49. Thomas Gray, *Scalachronica*, 110.

50. On this point Froissart offers the confounding description that the 'archers were formed up in the manner of a portcullis or harrow, and the men-at-arms in the rear' (Froissart, 164). However, in his description of the events of the battle, he reinforces le Baker's idea of a wing-like formation (le Baker, 44), writing that the earls of Alençon and Flanders, 'coasting, as it were, the archers, came to the prince's battalion'. (Froissart, 166.) They could hardly have 'coasted' a formation

composed of wedged pockets of archers. Le Bel writes only that the English were arrayed in three battles (le Bel, Rogers, *Sources*, 132).

51. Jim Bradbury, *The Medieval Archer* (New York: St Martin's Press, 1985), 95–9.

52. Michael Prestwich, 'The Battle of Crécy', in *The Battle of Crécy 1346*, Andrew Ayton and Sir Philip Preston (Rochester, New York: Boydell Press, 2005), 144. Prestwich goes on to point out that 'it is much more likely that a clerk, such as Froissart, would have this in mind, rather than an agricultural implement'.

53. Clifford Rogers, *War Cruel and Sharp*, 266–7.

54. Bradbury, 107.

55. Rogers, *War Cruel and Sharp*, 266–7.

56. Prestwich, 146.

57. Le Bel, 164.

58. Le Baker, 44.

59. Froissart, 166.

60. Le Baker (44) tells us that they were 'in the ground near their front line, each a foot deep and a foot wide, so that if the French cavalry approached, their horses would stumble in the pits'.

61. Froissart, 163.

62. Froissart, 163.

63. Jean le Bel, 'The Battle of Crécy', *Wars of Edward III*, 131–2.

64. Froissart, 164.

65. Le Bel, 132.

66. Le Bel, 132.

67. Froissart, 164–5. Knighton (63) confirms the story: 'There fell a flood of rain, with terrible thunder, but that amazing storm soon passed.' Le Bel does not mention the storm.

68. Prestwich doubts this explanation for the Genoese ineffectiveness ('Battle of Crécy', 148).

69. Froissart, 165–6.

70. Le Bel, 132. Froissart adds that Philip ordered that any man found retreating should be killed (Johnes, 166). Le Baker (43) reports that the French knights 'on young warhorses and agile chargers, rode down seven thousand of the crossbowmen who were between them and the English'.

71. Le Bel, 132.

72. Froissart, 166. Le Bel, 133.

73. Knighton, 63. Froissart, 167.

74. Le Bel, 133.

75. Froissart, 168.

76. Le Baker, 45. Edward III himself reported that 4,000 Frenchmen died in the pursuit ('King's Own Account', 131).

77. Capgrave, 212.

78. Knighton, 63–5.

79. Le Baker, 45.

80. Le Bel, 135.

81. Le Baker, 44.

82. William Pakington, *Neville's Cross*, in 'The Scottish Invasion of 1346', in *The Wars of Edward III*, ed. Clifford Rogers, 137. This chapter relies heavily upon two excellent histories of the battle, as follows. Clifford J. Rogers, 'The Scottish Invasion of 1346', *Northern History* XXXIV, 1998, 51–80. Kelly DeVries, *Infantry Warfare in the Fourteenth Century*, (Boydell and Brewer, 1996), 182–5.

83. Froissart, 173.

84. Jonathan Sumption, *Trial by Fire*, 34.

85. See *Wars of Edward III*, 148–51.

86. Chandos' Herald, lines 531–50.

87. Chandos' Herald, *Le Prince noir*, trans. Fransique Michel, lines 638–55.

88. Alfred Burne, *The Crécy War*, 253–4.

89. Barber, *Life and Campaigns of the Black Prince*, 52. The *écu* was the royal gold coin instituted by Louis IX and equivalent to the *livre* or pound.

90. 'The Prince of Wales Makes Preparations for a New Campaign' (Source: MS CCC78, fo. 179), Rogers, *The Wars of Edward III*, 162.

91. Froissart, 210.

92. Rogers, *War Cruel and Sharp*, 352.

93. Rogers, *War Cruel and Sharp*, 355.

94. Hewitt, 104.

95. Froissart, 210.

96. Michael Prestwich, *Armies and Warfare in the Middle Ages, the English Experience* (New Haven, Connecticut: Yale University Press 1996), 204.

97. Froissart, 272.

98. Chandos' Herald, lines 723–7.

99. Froissart, 99.

100. The chronicler (Froissart, 99) continues in describing the logistical dilemma even to the point of stating that the English 'much regretted that they had so thoroughly laid waste the land of Berry, Anjou and Touraine instead of gathering stores'.

101. Rogers, *War Cruel and Sharp*, 356–63.

102. 'Edward prince of Wales to the mayor, aldermen and commons of London, 22 October', Barber, 58.

103. H.J. Hewitt, *The Black Prince's Expedition* (Barnsley, South Yorkshire: Pen and Sword, 2004), 109–10.

104. *Anonimalle*, 165.

105. *Scalachronica*, 122.

106. Froissart, 100.

107. Though La Chaboterie is the generally accepted location of this skirmish, Rogers presents a convincing argument that Savigny-Lévescault is a more likely alternative (Rogers, *War Cruel and Sharp*, notes pp. 364–5). Not least of these points is that the Black Prince in his personal account of the battle describes the skirmish site as being three leagues (9 miles) from Chauvigny. Savigny-Lévescault is slightly more than 8½ miles from Chauvigny by road.

108. Froissart (100) lists among the captured knights 'Raoul de Courcy [...] Comte de Joigny, the Vicomte de Breuse, [and] the Seigneur de Chauvigny'. Le Baker (72) states that the Black Prince 'attacked the rear of the enemy army, capturing two counts, those of Joigny and Auxerre, and the Marshal of Burgundy. These were held for ransom, but a large number of men-at-arms were killed in the skirmish.' Sir Thomas Gray (*Scalachronica*, 122) lists: 'the Comtes d'Auxerre and de Joigny, and with them more than one hundred men-at-arms, knights and esquires'. The *Anonimalle Chronicle* (165) reports: 'The Counts of Auxerre, Sancerre, and Joigny were captured there, along with a good eight hundred men-at-arms, knights and esquires.' Sir Henry Knighton (143) offers no details of the engagement, but provides numbers closest to those of le Baker: 'On the Saturday before the battle [17 Sept. 1356] there were captured the count of Joigny, the count of Auxerre, and the Marshal of Burgundy, and 240 men-at-arms captured or slain.'

109. Froissart, 102.

110. Black Prince to Londoners, 58.

111. Le Baker, 72; Froissart, 100–2; *Anonimalle*, 165; *Scalachronica*, 122–3.

112. 'On Saturday [17 September] the English marched forward from prime to vespers, halting at a spot two short leagues from Poitiers.' (Froissart, 101–2.)

113. According to Sir Thomas Gray (*Scalachronica*, 123), 'The said Cardinal begged that [the Black Prince] would appoint nine of his people to treat with nine others of theirs, midway between the two armies, about a reasonable way to peace; which was arranged and performed; but it took no effect.' The *Anonimalle* (165) differs little from this: 'So they chose from the two sides 24 of the wisest men of the two armies, bishops, dukes, barons, counts and knights, twelve from each side. And so they negotiated for a truce all that Sunday, being in the open field all day as well as the following night, a bowshot's distance between the two armies.'

114. Chandos' Herald, lines 857–930.

115. John of Fordun, *Chronicle of the Scottish Nation*, ed. W.F. Skene., tr. F.J.H. Skene (Edinburgh: Edmonston and Douglas, 1872).

116. Le Baker, *Campaigns of the Black Prince*, 73. Froissart (104), however, credits Sir Eustace de Ribemont with concocting the plan.

117. Le Baker, 73. Froissart (104) confirms this course of action, having Jean order the select horsemen to 'break through the lines of archers for your own battalions to follow in quickly'. Other sources do not comment on the French plan.

Notes and Sources

118. Henry Dwight Sedgwick, *The Life of Edward the Black Prince, 1330–1376* (Indianapolis: Bobbs-Merrill Co., 1932), 127. Similarly, Oman calls the French plan 'absolutely insane' (*Art of War*, 130).

119. Chandos' Herald, 143.

120. Chandos' Herald, 143.

121. Knighton (143) writes that Jean ordered that only the Black Prince was to be spared. Also, Froissart (103) confirms that Charny carried the *oriflamme*.

122. Le Baker, 74.

123. *The Chronicle of Jean de Venette*, ed. Austin P. Evans (New York: Columbia University Press, 1953), 64.

124. Froissart, 102.

125. Chandos, 144.

126. John of Fordun.

127. Froissart, 102; le Baker, 74.

128. Chandos, 142.

129. Froissart, 107.

130. Froissart, 107.

131. Chandos' Herald, lines 855–6.

132. Froissart, 106.

133. Le Baker, 73.

134. Froissart, 107.

135. Chandos, 141.

136. Knighton, 143.

137. Froissart, 108.

138. Le Baker, 74.

139. Le Baker, 73.

140. *Scalachronica*, 123.

141. Malmesbury, *Eulogium historiarum* (III, 223) tr. Alfred Burne, 'The Battle of Poitiers', *EHR* 43 (1938), 25.

142. There exist several striking similarities between the battles of Halidon Hill and Poitiers, as shall become obvious to the reader. The key point at this moment, however, is while most sources agree that both the Scots and the English army each contained three divisions, it is possible that a fourth English division under Edward Balliol formed on the field to the rear of the three primary battalions. 'The English, like the Scots, were arrayed in three divisions, and the king of Scotland [Edward Balliol] was in the rear battalion.' (*Chronicle of Lanercost*, II, 279.) Historian Kelly DeVries briefly addresses the controversy in *Infantry Warfare in the Early Fourteenth Century* (Rochester, New York: Boydell Press, 1996), notes 122.

143. Froissart, 103, Folio Society, 1966.

144. '[Sir James Audley] rode off ahead of the other knights to engage with the battalion of the marshals of France, falling in with Sir Arnoul d'Audrehem and his company

[...] Very soon after Sir Eustace had been taken the battle began on all fronts, firstly where the battalion of the marshals, riding ahead of those whose task was to destroy the English archers [...] for by now the marshals' battalion was being harried and put to rout by the archers ...' (Froissart, 110–12].

145. Ed. Rogers. *Anonimalle*, 166.

146. 'Ensement a li nobles Rois Jehans ordene ses courrous, en le quarte bataille fu ...' (Chandos' Herald, 30).

147. 'The Kyng of Frauns had IIII. Batayles.' John Capgrave, *Chronicle of England*, ed. Francis Charles Hingeston (London: Longman, Brown, Green, Longmans, and Roberts, 1858), 217.

148. *Chronique des quatre premiers Valois*, 1.

149. 'Et ex parte Francorum, duo marescalli Francie habuerunt primam acie. Secundum aciem dominus Dolfynus de Vienna, dum fratre suo duce de Orlyons cum maiori fortitudine. In tercia acie erat rex Francie ...' *Knighton's Chronicle, 1337–1396*, ed. and trans. G.H. Martin (New York: Oxford University Press, 1995), 142–3.

150. Le Baker (76–9) has the marshals commanding the first battalion, the Dauphin the second, and King Jean the third.

151. Le Baker, 78.

152. Chandos' Herald, 143.

153. Chandos' Herald, 146. Froissart (110) cites a similar story about James Audley's vow, though the chronology is different; Froissart has the request made at the very beginning of the fight, just as the French marshals attack. He also reports that 'with the prince, to guard and advise him, was Sir John Chandos, and whatever was happening he did not leave him throughout the day. Lord James Audley was also with the prince for a great part of the time.' Further into the fight, this point is re-emphasized (Froissart, 116): 'there beside the prince to hold his bridle were Sir John Chandos and Sir Peter Audley, brother of Lord James Audley'. Among Bartholomew Burghersh's dispatch, the *Anonimalle Chronicle*, Knighton and le Baker, none relates the vow story, but the last (le Baker, 82) does attest to Sir James' valour, which he reports both the Black Prince and King Jean acknowledge.

154. Chandos' Herald, 143.

155. Froissart, 111.

156. Froissart, 114.

157. Froissart, 111. The marshals' mission is also described in le Baker (76) when he writes about Clermont's troop specifically, stating that they were: 'designed to ride down the archers and protect their companions from them'.

158. Sir Thomas Gray, *Scalachronica*, 124.

159. *Chronique des quatre premiers Valois*, tr. Rogers, 2.

160. Froissart, 105.

161. Froissart, 104.

162. Chandos' Herald, lines 995–6.

Notes and Sources

163. For a brief but excellent discussion of French tactical innovations made during the period between the two battles, see T.F. Tout's 'Some Neglected Fights between the Battles of Crecy and Poitiers', in *English Historical Review*, 20:80 (1905), 726–30.
164. Le Baker, 75–6.
165. At dawn on Monday 'the Earl of Warwick crossed a narrow causeway over a marsh where he found a French town with a castle'. (*Anonimalle*, 166.)
166. Froissart, 102.
167. Black Prince to Londoners, 58.
168. *Anonimalle*, 165.
169. Froissart refers to separate English battalions at different points, but does not ever refer to the Earls of Warwick or Salisbury anywhere in his account of the battle, nor does Thomas Gray (*Scalachronica*, 143–4). The former chronicler seemed far more concerned with the individual acts of valour by such knights as Chandos, Audley and d'Aubrecicourt. Le Baker (72) reports initially that the Earls of Warwick and Oxford jointly commanded the vanguard, the prince the centre, and the Earls of Salisbury and Suffolk the rear. When describing the actions of the battle, however, he credits Warwick and Salisbury with independent command of their respective divisions, as does Chandos' Herald (144–5), and the *Anonimalle Chronicle* (165–6). Henry Knighton (143) mentions only that Warwick commanded the van. John of Fordun (*Chronicle of the Scottish Nation*), writing for a Scottish audience, mentions only Sir William Douglas by name. Only *Chronique des quatre premiers Valois* suggests an almost entirely original organization. In the *Chronique*, the first division, which reportedly contained the archers, is commanded by Sir Hugh Caveley, Sir Edmund Warwick, the Lord Lucy, Nicholas Dagworth, Sir John Pipe and Sir John Jewel. The second, Gascon, division, was commanded by the Lord of Albret, the Lord of Pommiers, Sir Edmond de Pommiers and the Captal de Buch. The prince commanded the third division, accompanied by Sir John de Montfort, Sir William d'Anselles and Sir John Chandos.
170. Froissart, 104.
171. Froissart, 104.
172. Froissart, 109.
173. Froissart, 109.
174. 'All Sunday they worked to the completion of their defences, and spent it as well as they could in strengthening their positions with ditches, round which they posted their archers.' (Froissart, 108.)
175. *Anonimalle*, 166.
176. *Scalachronica*, 123.
177. *Scalachronica*, 123–4. Also, Froissart, 108–9: 'About sunrise the cardinal renewed his journeying from one camp to the other, and thought that by his negotiations he could bring them to terms, but he could not, for the French angrily told him to go to Poitiers or anywhere else he chose and give up acting as peacemaker, for he was

likely to bring disaster on himself. The cardinal, who was seeking only to do good, did not wish to run further into danger and took his leave of the king of France, for he saw that he was labouring in vain.'

178. *Anonimalle*, 166.
179. Hewitt (118–19), on this point, states that he will be brief, but is also non-committal. He writes that 'It is now generally accepted that it was intended to be the first phase of a retreat, if retreat should prove to be practicable. Yet it is possible to see in the movement a feint and to regard the French command as deceived.' He does not, however, admit allegiance to either belief.
180. Barber, 141.
181. Burne notes that the truce was to end at 7.30 on Monday morning (Burne, 300). Hewitt (119) reports that the sun rose that day at 5.45.
182. Rogers, *War Cruel and Sharp*, 372.
183. Froissart, 109. *Scalachronica*, 124.
184. Le Baker, 76.
185. Rogers, *War Cruel and Sharp*, notes, 377.
186. Le Baker, 75.
187. Le Baker, 76.
188. *Anonimalle*, 166. Emphasis added.
189. Le Baker, 76.
190. Froissart, 109.
191. Le Baker, 75.
192. *Anonimalle*, 166.
193. Chandos' Herald, lines 1103–12.
194. Froissart, 110.
195. Froissart, 110.
196. Froissart, 110.
197. 'Likewise on the other side Sir Eustace d'Aubrecicourt [...] had taken great pains to be among the first in the attack, where indeed he was at the very moment when Lord James was advancing to seek his enemies.' (Froissart, 110–11.)
198. Chandos' Herald, lines 1113–15.
199. Froissart, 111.
200. Froissart, 111.
201. Froissart, 114.
202. Froissart, 106.
203. Chandos' Herald, lines 1129–56.
204. *Chronique des quatre premiers Valois*, tr. Clifford Rogers, 2.
205. Le Baker, 74.
206. Le Baker, 75–6.
207. Le Baker, 76. Chandos' Herald (lines 1163–71) confirms that the English rearguard was the first to counter the French attack.

Notes and Sources

208. Froissart, 111.

209. Le Baker (76) writes that 'Clermont was eager to clear himself of any earlier imputations'.

210. John of Fordun.

211. *Chronique des quatre premiers Valois*, tr. Clifford Rogers, 2.

212. *Anonimalle*, 166.

213. Richard Barber, *Edward, Prince of Wales and Aquitaine* (New York: Charles Scribner's Sons, 1978), Map, page 140.

214. Barber, 141.

215. Le Baker, 76.

216. Barber, 141–2.

217. Le Baker, 76.

218. Froissart, 105.

219. 'Clermont, fighting bravely, met a not unavenged death, disdaining flight or surrender. D'Audrehem was forced to flee.' (Le Baker, 77.) 'The Marshal d'Audrehem bore himself very well and with boldness, but was compelled to retreat.' (*Chronique des quatre premiers Valois*, tr. Clifford Rogers, 2.)

220. Froissart, 111–12.

221. Le Baker, 77.

222. Le Baker, 76.

223. Froissart, 112.

224. Le Baker, 76–7.

225. Le Baker, 77.

226. Chandos' Herald, lines 1205–26.

227. Le Baker, 77.

228. *Chronique des quatre premiers Valois*, tr. Rogers, 3. The *Chronique* is clear on this point, but differs from other sources with regard to the sequence of the French divisions. According to the *Chronique*, the Duke of Orléans (King Jean's brother) led the second division, and the Dauphin the third (2–3). If this inconsistency is overlooked, the source proves useful because of its other details that explain the flow of events better than do some of the other chronicles.

229. Froissart, 114.

230. *Chronique des quatre premiers Valois*, tr. Rogers, 2.

231. 'And the noble Prince of England joined his division with the division of the Dauphin of Vienne and the two brothers, the Dukes of Anjou and Berry, striking and fighting with them, and in the end defeating them.' (*Anonimalle*, 166.)

232. *Chronique des quatre premiers Valois*, tr. Rogers, 2.

233. Chandos' Herald, line 1234; Le Baker, 77; Froissart, 112.

234. Le Baker, 78.

235. Froissart, 112.

236. Froissart, 113.

237. Le Baker, 78.
238. *Anonimalle*, 166.
239. John of Fordun.
240. *Chronique des quatre premiers Valois*, tr. Rogers, 3.
241. Froissart, 114.
242. Chandos' Herald, lines 1236–8.
243. *Anonimalle*, 166.
244. Froissart, 115.
245. Froissart, 115.
246. *Anonimalle*, 166.
247. Le Baker, 78.
248. Chandos' Herald, lines 1247–8, 1259.
249. Le Baker, 77–8.
250. Knighton, 145.
251. *Chronique des quatre premiers Valois*, tr. Rogers, 2.
252. Le Baker, 78.
253. Froissart, 115.
254. Knighton, 145.
255. The *Anonimalle Chronicle* (166) numbers the king's 'division' at '8,000 bascinets, along with a great number of shieldbearers, crossbowmen, and other infantry.' Froissart (115, 117) describes the king as being armed with a battleaxe. Le Baker (80–1) does not specify the weapon Jean used, but makes a point of saying that he beheaded some men during the fight, which would not necessarily be an exaggeration if the king did have an axe.
256. Knighton, 145.
257. *Anonimalle*, 166.
258. Froissart, 112.
259. Le Baker, 78.
260. Le Baker, 79. Hewitt (130), however, disputes Woodland's role as standard-bearer, naming instead Walter Shank to that position of honour. Barber (143) does not accept Hewitt's proposal.
261. Froissart, 113. Chandos' Herald adds: 'Let each one take heed to his honour!' (Lines 1276–7.)
262. Froissart, 115.
263. Le Baker, 79.
264. Le Baker, 79.
265. *Chronique Valois*, 3.
266. Le Baker, 79.
267. Knighton, 145.
268. Oman, *The Art of War in the Middle Ages*, 130; Alfred Burne, *The Crecy War*, (Eyre & Spottiswoode, 1955, Wordsworth, 1999), 305–6; Jonathan Sumption, *The Hundred*

Notes and Sources

Years War, vol. II: Trial by Fire (Philadelphia: University of Pennsylvania Press, 1999), 242; H.J. Hewitt, *The Black Prince's Expedition.*

269. Jim Bradbury, *The Medieval Archer* (New York: St Martin's Press, 1985), 109.
270. Burne, a British lieutenant colonel, referred to his system as 'Inherent Military Probability' and used it throughout his works to conjecture otherwise indeterminable tactical details of historical situations.
271. *Anonimalle*, 166.
272. Le Baker, 75.
273. Le Baker, 79.
274. Le Baker, 79.
275. Burne, 299; Sumption, 243.
276. Le Baker, 79.
277. *Anonimalle*, 166.
278. Le Baker, 80.
279. *Chronique Valois*, 3.
280. Froissart, 115.
281. Venette, 64.
282. Le Baker, 80–1.
283. *Chronique Valois*, 3.
284. Le Baker, 81.
285. Chandos' Herald, lines 1351–3.
286. Barber, 59.
287. Froissart, 118.
288. Froissart, 120.
289. Le Baker, 81.
290. Froissart, 119–20.
291. Knighton, 145–7.
292. Knighton, 149.
293. *Anonimalle*, 166. Sumption settled on 3,000 captured, including '1,400 belted knights'. (*Trial by Fire*, 247.)
294. Froissart, 121.
295. Burghersh, 163.
296. Burghersh, 164.
297. 'The Frensch fled, the Kyng was take, and Philippe his yonger son, James Borbon, and XI. erles, the bischop of Senonensis, with other lordis and knytes to the noumbyr of too thousand. There were killed too dukes, XIX. Lords, and five thousand of men of armes, beside other puple.' (Capgrave, 217.)
298. 'When they were all collected, they found they had twice as many prisoners as themselves.' (Froissart, v1, tr. Thomas Johnes, 225.)
299. Froissart (109) had numbered the French at 50,000.
300. Chandos' Herald, lines 1370–4, 1387.

301. Hewitt (136) reaches the same conclusion: 'The king was still on French soil and quite near at hand. The proper course for the Order of the Star was to rescue the king.'
302. Froissart, 225–6.
303. *Chronique Valois*, 3.
304. Burne, 313–14. Among the obvious difficulties here we must include his assumptions that (1) Not a single man in the Duke of Orléans' division was wounded, killed, captured, or joined Jean for the final attack, and (2) That 80 per cent of the wounded escaped capture and only one half of those captured were wounded first. By his math 2,500 were killed, 2,000 captured, and 5,000 wounded, for a total of 9,500 killed, wounded, and captured. Burne, though precise in his explanation of how he arrived at the estimate, somehow came up with 8,500 as a total. Burne's three other calculations of the French totals are equally dubious.
305. Sumption, *Trial by Fire*, 247; Rogers, *War Cruel and Sharp*, 384.
306. Hewitt, 137. Sumption, however, accepts the report of forty dead English men-at-arms (*Trial by Fire*, 246).
307. Froissart (Johnes), 227; Knighton, 145–9.
308. Hewitt, 137.
309. Chandos' Herald, 'Et quant ce vint au grant matyn,' line 1103.
310. Froissart (Johnes), 225.
311. Burne, 300.
312. *Trial by Fire*, 245.
313. *Trial by Fire*, 242.
314. Le Baker, 81.
315. Le Baker, 81.
316. Froissart (Johnes), 226.
317. Le Baker, 81.
318. Le Baker, 81.
319. Froissart (Johnes), 225; Le Baker, 81.
320. Though Chandos' Herald calls it 'un petit pavillon', line 1438.
321. Froissart (Johnes), 224–5; Le Baker, 81–2.
322. Froissart (Johnes), 225.
323. Froissart (Johnes), 226.
324. Le Baker 82; Froissart (Johnes), 226–7; Chandos' Herald, lines 1415–34.
325. Froissart (Johnes), 226–7.
326. *Trial by Fire*, 248. Historian Chris Given-Wilson, however, argues that many of the hostages defaulted on their ransoms, decreasing their monetary value, but that their true value lay in the political capital they brought their captors. 'Edward III's Prisoners of War: the Battle of Poitiers and its Context', *EHR* 116:468 (2001): 826–30.
327. Froissart, 228.
328. Chandos' Herald, lines 1493–1515.

Notes and Sources

329. Froissart, 230–1.

330. *Scalachronica*, in Clifford Rogers' *The Wars of Edward III*, 168–9.

331. Capgrave, *Capgrave's Chronicle of England*, 220.

332. 'The Ravages of War', in *Wars of Edward III*, 169.

333. H.J. Hewitt, 144.

334. Knighton, 151–5. See Rogers, 'Bergerac', *JMMH2*, 107–8.

335. 'The Treaty of Berwick, 1357,' in *English Historical Documents, IV 1327–1485* (New York: Oxford University Press, 1969), 101–3.

336. Clifford Rogers, *War Cruel and Sharp*, 387. This assessment of the French view of the proposal is in line with Delachenal's reading of the *Chronique Normande*, but le Patourel suggests that the Dauphin was perhaps less enthusiastic. Le Patourel, 'Treaty of Brétigny, 1360', *Transactions of the Royal Historical Society*, 5:10 (1960), 27.

337. For more discussion of the papal conflicts, see Rogers, *War Cruel and Sharp*, 386–8.

338. 'The First Treaty of London' in *Sources*, 170–1.

339. Christopher Allmand, *The Hundred Years War* (New York: Cambridge University Press, 1988), 19.

340. Le Patourel, 28.

341. For an in-depth discussion of Charles' defection, see Sumption, *Trial by Fire*, 418–21.

342. 'Rejection of the Second Treaty of London', in *Wars of Edward III*, 172–3.

343. *War Cruel and Sharp*, 398–9.

344. 'The Start of the 1359 Campaign', in *Wars of Edward III*, 175–6.

345. 'From Rheims to Paris', in *Wars of Edward III*, 176–80.

346. *Trial by Fire*, 438. For detailed and on some points vastly differing interpretations of the 1359–1360 campaign and the Treaty of Brétigny, see Rogers, *War Cruel and Sharp*, 385–422; and Sumption, *Trial by Fire*, 405–54.

347. *War Cruel and Sharp*, 416.

348. Le Patourel, 21.

349. Andrew of Wyntoun, *Wyntoun's Original Chronicle*, VI. ed. F.J. Amours (London: William Blackwood and Sons, 1908), 227, lines 6822–3.

350. Chandos' Herald, lines 3385–6.

Index

Victory at Poitiers